DRUKPA KUNLEY

Advance Praise for *Drukpa Kunley: Sacred Tales of a Mad Monk*

'The medieval mystic Drukpa Kunley is loved and revered across the Himalaya. Needrup Zangpo's work brings his magical and profound philosophy as a gift and benediction to readers.'

—Namita Gokhale, author and festival director

'Unfamiliar to most Westerners, Drukpa Kunley, the divine madman of Bhutan, is the most picaresque of the Dharma Lords. Under the appearance of a collection of tales and legends, this book is an invitation to discover his mischievous and yet most profound mind.'

—Dr Thierry Mathou, Ambassador of France to India

'*Drukpa Kunley: Sacred Tales of a Mad Monk* explores Bhutanese culture through thirty-three tales of Lam Drukpa Kunley, a sixteenth-century figure known as the Divine Madman. Needrup Zangpo skilfully employs creative non-fiction to narrate the Tibetan Buddhist master's visits to Bhutan, where the latter challenged religious dogma and societal hypocrisy. In an era of heightened political correctness, this well-researched anthology, written in both Dzongkha and English, offers a timely perspective. Accompanied by captivating illustrations, the book provides an insightful look at a historical figure, making it both informative and engaging.'

—Tshering Tashi, writer and festival director, Bhutan Echoes

DRUKPA
SACRED TALES OF A MAD MONK
KUNLEY

NEEDRUP ZANGPO

Foreword by JIGME TENZIN WANGPO
Introduction by DR KARMA PHUNTSHO

HarperCollins *Publishers* India

First published in India by HarperCollins *Publishers* 2025
4th Floor, Tower A, Building No. 10, DLF Cyber City,
DLF Phase II, Gurugram, Haryana – 122002
www.harpercollins.co.in

2 4 6 8 10 9 7 5 3 1

Copyright © Needrup Zangpo 2025

Illustrations courtesy Chimi R. Namgyal,
21st Century Illusion, crnamgyal@gmail.com

P-ISBN: 978-93-6569-378-2
E-ISBN: 978-93-6569-597-7

The views and opinions expressed in this book are the author's own
and the facts are as reported by him, and the publishers
are not in any way liable for the same.

Needrup Zangpo asserts the moral right
to be identified as the author of this work.

All rights reserved. No part of this publication may be reproduced,
stored in a retrieval system, or transmitted, in any form or by any means,
electronic, mechanical, photocopying, recording or otherwise,
without the prior permission of the publishers.

Typeset in 11.5/15.6 Adobe Caslon Pro at
HarperCollins *Publishers* India

Printed and bound at
Replika Press Pvt. Ltd.

MIX
Paper | Supporting
responsible forestry
FSC
www.fsc.org FSC™ C016779

This book is produced from independently certified FSC® paper to ensure
responsible forest management.

To my beloved son and daughter, Nyungpo and Numo

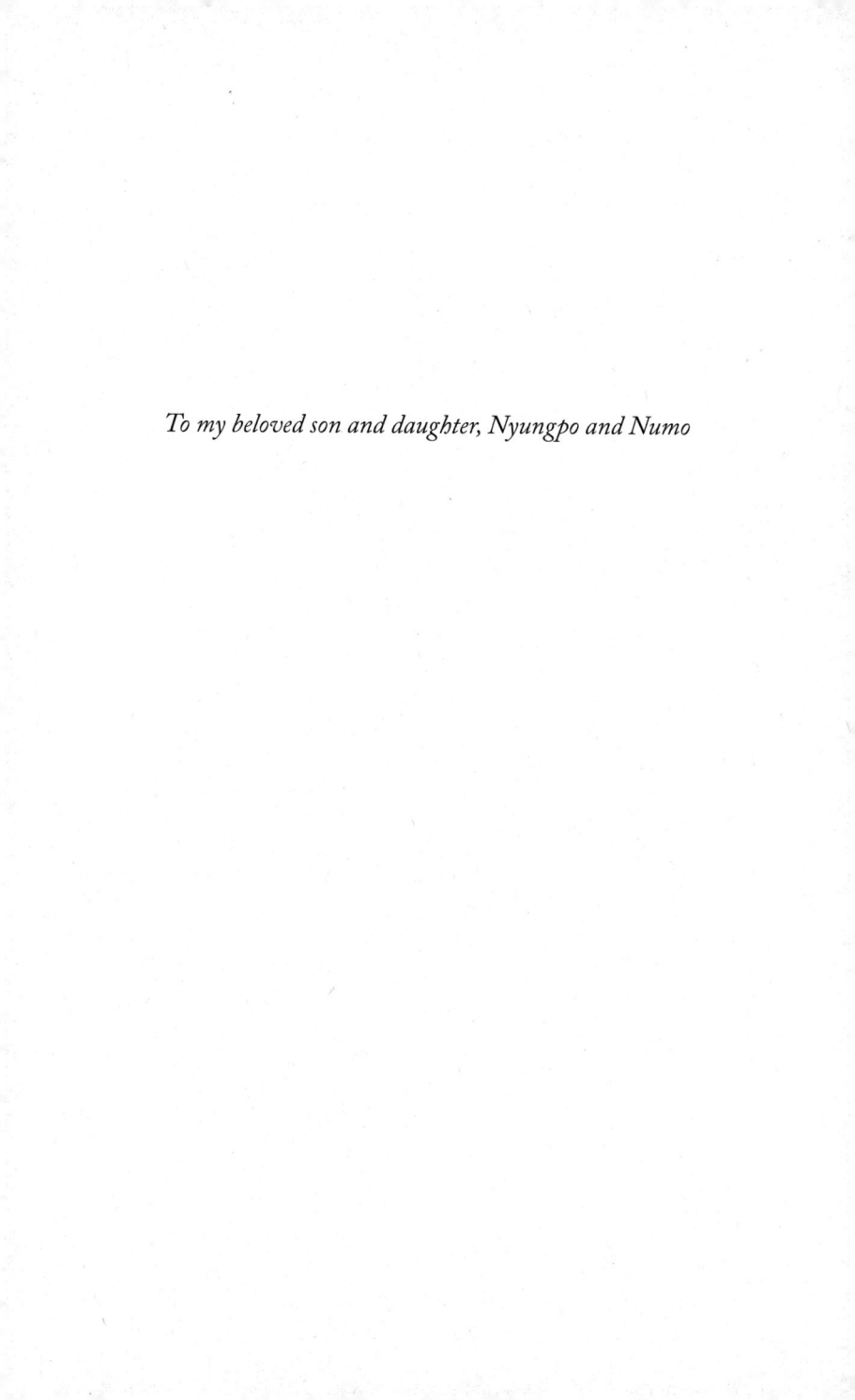

Contents

Foreword	ix
Introduction	xi
Preface	xxv
Prologue	xxxix
1. The Flight of the Messenger Arrow	1
2. An Egg-Headed Beast to the Rescue	8
3. The Demoness Who Wears a Skin Dress	12
4. Arresting the Sun's Descent to Build a Stupa	15
5. Shooting a Devotee Dead	20
6. The Undertaker Who Walks a Corpse to the Cremation Ground	25
7. A Hammer that Inflicts a Rotting Wound	32
8. The Burial of Dochula's Terror	38
9. The Deliverance of Wola Gyap Tenzin	43
10. The Birth of the Goat-Headed Bull	52
11. The Mad Yogi Who Urinated Gold	62
12. When a Wanderer Meets a Treasure Revealer	66
13. If You Persist, Even Your Mother Relents	74
14. Philandering Nuns' Paternity Claim Refuted	78

15.	Beyond Dress and Appearance	82
16.	No Virtuous Abbot for Dechenphu	89
17.	Wager Not Your Fish Away	95
18.	When Karmapa was Smitten by Beauty	100
19.	Jamtrul's Donkey Incarnate	104
20.	Sacha's Girl and the Dawn Within	108
21.	The Burden of Breaking a Bow and Ploughshare	113
22.	Subduing Fearsome Spears and Dogs	117
23.	Breaking Ngawang Chogyal's Shackles of Avarice	121
24.	A Herd of Meat for Tsang Desi	126
25.	Prostrating to Palkhor Stupa and the Gyangtse Girl	130
26.	Entrusting Old Shoes to Jowo Shakyamuni	136
27.	Monks Steal Drukpa Kunley's Afflictive Emotions	141
28.	The Farting Metaphysicist and Tsongkhapa	146
29.	Drukpa's Loud-Voiced Friend	151
30.	The Miracle Behind Trashi Lhunpo's Famed Tea	154
31.	No Place is Safe without Self-Restraint	158
32.	When a Snobbish Family Saw Excrement for Tormas	166
33.	To Earn the Worth of Ponies and Pussies	170
	Epilogue	175
	Acknowledgements	177
	Index	179

དཔལ་ལྡན་འབྲུག་པའི་ཆོས་སྡེ།
གསང་ཆེན་རྡོ་རྗེ་ཐེག་པའི་སློབ་སྦྱོང་སྒྲིག་གཞི།
རྟ་མགོ་ཆོས་དབྱིངས་ཕོ་བྲང་།

Institute for Vajrayana Studies
Tago choeying Phodrang

Date:16/06/2024

Foreword

It is with great pleasure that I introduce *Drukpa Kunley: Sacred Tales of a Mad Monk* by Needrup Zangpo. This anthology marks a significant milestone in Bhutanese literature, as it is the first book in English on Drukpa Kunley written by a Bhutanese author who has grown up hearing and reading his stories. I am delighted that this book is being published by HarperCollins, a prestigious international publishing house that will undoubtedly help bring Drukpa Kunley's remarkable legacy to a wider readership.

With his profound fascination with and keen interest in Drukpa Kunley's tales, Needrup Zangpo brings a unique authenticity and intimacy to these stories that only a native voice could offer. Drukpa Kunley, the revered mad yogi, left an indelible mark on Bhutanese culture through his unconventional and profound deeds. His legacy, preserved in literature, folklore, and teachings, continues to inspire and intrigue.

The thirty-three stories in this collection serve as testament to his greatness. They are based on biographical narratives in Classical Tibetan and oral tales passed down through generations. The effort and dedication that have gone into the creation of this anthology are commendable. Needrup Zangpo's meticulous research and thoughtful storytelling shine through on every page.

He has succeeded in maintaining the essence of Drukpa Kunley's wisdom and wit while presenting the stories in a contemporary idiom that will resonate with a global readership. This is no small feat, and it underscores the significance of this work not only for Bhutanese literature but also for the broader understanding of Himalayan culture and spirituality.

Needrup Zangpo's achievement in retelling these stories with such clarity and simplicity is truly praiseworthy. It is a proud moment for Bhutan. I commend Needrup Zangpo for his dedication and skill in bringing the mad yogi's adventures to life for readers around the world.

May these stories inspire, enlighten and entertain, just as they have done for generations in Bhutan.

Jigme Tenzin Wangpo
Gyelsay Trulku

P.O. Box No. 324   Tel No. 00975-02-36282,   Fax No. 361313

Introduction

Dr Karma Phuntsho

Drukpa Kunley, whose life and travels are recounted in this book, is one of the most well-known and most-loved religious figures in Bhutan. His stories abound in Bhutanese society, both to entertain and inspire people. Yet, the real Drukpa Kunley remains a very elusive figure. Portrayals of him in his own autobiographical accounts and songs differ from those in later biographies and the oral stories told of him in the Buddhist Himalayas. He is referred to with different titles such as religious lord (choje), accomplished saint (drubthob), madman (myonpa), yogi (naljorpa) and carefree vagrant (byatang), and described variously as a savant, ascetic, wandering mendicant, miracle man, philanderer, drunkard, social critic, sublime master and a buddha. Who was Drukpa Kunley then?

Before discussing the differences in these presentations and the roles he played, it is pertinent to lay to rest a couple of major misconceptions concerning his identity. Drukpa Kunley, the madman of Druk, was not Bhutanese, as some may be inclined to believe, given his name. The state of Bhutan as we know today was yet to be formed during his time. He was from Ralung, the main centre of the Drukpa Kagyu tradition in southern Tibet, and the name 'Drukpa' in his days referred to the followers of the

Drukpa Kagyu school. It would take at least three more centuries for the name to be used to refer to the citizens of the Bhutanese territory.

Similarly, the depiction of Drukpa Kunley as the patron saint of Bhutan by some writers is, at best, naïve and inaccurate, lacking a nuanced cultural understanding and use of language. Drukpa Kunley does not play any significant role of protection and intercession in the Bhutanese religious culture, as a patron saint would be generally expected to. His influence on Bhutan's religious consciousness and culture is dwarfed by figures such as Padmasambhava (eighth century), the saint who is credited with the introduction of Buddhism to Bhutan, and Zhabdrung Ngawang Namgyal (1594–1651), one of Drukpa Kunley's relatives who launched the process of unifying the Bhutanese valleys into one state in the seventeenth century. The Bhutanese chant many supplications and prayers on a daily basis to these two figures and regard them as spiritual paragons, but most Bhutanese hardly know a prayer to Drukpa Kunley or celebrate him as a spiritual guardian or religious leader. Unlike Padmasambhava or Zhabdrung, there is not a single day or occasion in the Bhutanese calendar dedicated to Drukpa Kunley.

Yet, these facts do not diminish Drukpa Kunley's popularity among the Bhutanese as a spiritual adept, religious prankster, divine madman and incisive critic. He is enormously loved as a spiritual man with no hang-ups, prejudices or limitations, and a master of outstanding wit, humour, wisdom and magical power. Places, peoples and stories associated with him still thrive in Bhutan, particularly in the western valleys that he frequented during his lifetime. In these areas, there is an abundance of attention to his life story and legacies through associated temple sites, religious institutions, written stories, oral accounts, films and artefacts—the most pervasive of them being the phalluses painted on walls, hanging from the roof or sold as souvenirs to tourists.

Where do these diverse representations and characterizations of Drukpa Kunley come from and what are we to make of them in understanding the person himself? The most reliable sources to understand the historical figure Drukpa Kunley are his own autobiographical accounts and songs. These are contained in four works that were published some decades after him in Dreulhey in southern Tibet by the hierarch who was considered to be his reincarnation. These four works were produced from xylographic prints in the traditional loose-leaf *poti* format as a set. The set was reproduced in India in 1978 as the book *The Life Story, Songs and Advices of Drukpa Kunley*[1] and can be now found online at the Buddhist Digital Resource Centre with the identification number W1KG10253.

The first book contains sporadic accounts of Drukpa Kunley's life written in the first person and the three subsequent books are made up of his songs, satire, poems, letters, anecdotes and advice, which his students recorded and which were put together by his reincarnation. Several modern scholars, including R.A. Stein, E. Gene Smith, John Ardussi and more recently, Elizabeth Monson, have studied these books and written about them.

These books present Drukpa Kunley as a person with great erudition and penetrating insight into contemporary social and religious systems. Born in a collateral line of the Drukpa family in Ralung, he had a happy childhood, which abruptly ended with the death of his father in a feud over family estates. Following this, he served the Tibetan ruler Kuntu Zangpo (fifteenth century) at

---

1 (འབྲུག་པ་ཀུན་དགའ་ལེགས་པའི་རྣམ་ཐར་དང་ཉམས་མགུར་དང་ཞལ་གདམས་སོགས་)

the Rinpungpa court for six years, where he witnessed much strife over political power and control. By then, his mother had married his uncle who had earlier instigated the death of his father.

Disillusioned with worldly life by this sad turn of events, his thoughts turned to religion in his late teens. He became a peripatetic student and studied under numerous masters from different traditions. He was a fast learner and could memorize many pages of scriptures every morning and understand their content, while also applying them in practice. His scholarly acumen can be gauged from the very sharp and incisive critique he wrote later of the institutional and religious hypocrisies of his time, the comments he made on philosophical and religious topics and the highly engaging and humorous songs he sang on different occasions.

Although a vagabond, Drukpa Kunley had a very rich social and spiritual life and he mixed with the important figures of his time. He was close to the Rinpungpa rulers Kuntu Zangpo and Donyo Dorje (1463–1512) and often met important religious hierarchs such as the seventh Karmapa Chodrak Gyatso (1454–1506). It is probable that being a scion of the respectable Gya family of Ralung helped him make these connections, but Drukpa Kunley's presence was perhaps also appreciated for his honest, independent and open mind and sharp wit, which he shared with no selfish interest or agenda. In Bhutan, he appears to have known the local chieftains and leading lamas in the western valleys of Paro, Thimphu and Punakha. On his visit to Bumthang, perhaps his only trip east of Pelela pass, which he made directly from southern Tibet, he met the treasure discoverer Pema Lingpa (1450–1521), the foremost religious figure from the area of Bhutan with a large following in Tibet at the time. In Pema Lingpa, Drukpa Kunley may have found a good conversation partner who shared his spiritual sophistication and maverick character.

However, unlike Pema Lingpa, Drukpa Kunley was not interested in institutionalized religion and a monastic career. He roamed as a carefree mendicant with no permanent base or affiliation. According to his own description of his personality, 'he would go even as he wished to stay and stay even as he wished to go. He would not listen to anyone and not get along with anyone'. Wandering freely and uninhibited, he quickly gained a reputation as Druknyon or the 'Madman of Druk', one of the three famous madmen of his time. The other two madmen were Kunga Zangpo (1458–1532), the madman of Ue, and Heruka Rupi Gyenchen (1452–1507), the madman of Tsang. There were also others before and after them who called themselves madmen, but the 'madmen movement' perhaps reached its climax during Drukpa Kunley's time, although it remained only in the periphery of mainstream religious institutions.

Styled on the mahasiddha figures of India, the madmen were spiritual adepts known for their unprejudiced and uninhibited wisdom and outrageous behaviour. However, the holy madmen were hardly 'mad'. In fact, from their enlightened perspective, the rest of the world was utterly mad and intoxicated by bewildering thoughts and emotions. They remained in the state of non-dual awareness with no conceptual construction and defiling emotions. They had transcended the madness of the world to see through the deceptions but were called madmen for their unconventional behaviour that defied established norms and customs.

Drukpa Kunley is believed to have reached the great heights of spiritual realization to see through the vanity of life and the meaninglessness of worldly pursuits of happiness. He was seen as a spiritual man who was free of worldly concerns and had fully realized the uncontrived, open and empty nature of all things. Thus, at the core of his maverick character and antinomian behaviour is the realization of the ultimate reality of all things. This unrestrained awareness of reality, which defies all worldly logic and conventions, is put in the modern idiom as crazy wisdom. It is a state where one is completely free from the constraints of ego, hope and fear.

To the Bhutanese, Drukpa Kunley was a crazy-wisdom master par excellence. The second set of sources on Drukpa Kunley's life and works, coming mainly from Bhutanese authors, highlight and elaborate this aspect of Drukpa Kunley's fascinating character. The first Bhutanese biography of Drukpa Kunley was compiled in the sixteenth century by Tshewang Tenzin of Tango, who was considered to be Drukpa Kunley's son or grandson from his affair with the Bhutanese lady Pelzang Butri. Although the book titled *The Biography of Lord Kunga Lekpa Including His Deeds in Mon Paro*[2] is presented in the first person, it is a later compilation of what are mainly accounts of Drukpa Kunley's miraculous acts, which were perhaps passed down orally.

This account is further elaborated and embellished by Gendün Rinchen (1926-97), the sixty-ninth Je Khenpo of Bhutan, in his work published in 1971 titled *Meaningful to Behold: An Essence of the Ocean of the Life Stories of the Dharma Lord Kunga Lekpa*[3]. Using his literary deftness, Gendün Rinchen turned the accounts into highly entertaining and rousing stories and took the popularity of Drukpa Kunley to new heights. His work was

---

2 (འབྲུག་པའི་མགོན་པོ་ཀུན་དགའ་ལེགས་པའི་རྣམ་ཐར་མོན་སྤྲོ་སྒོ་སོགས་ཀྱི་མཛད་སྤྱོད་རྣམས་)

3 (འབྲུག་པའི་མགོན་པོ་ཆོས་རྗེ་ཀུན་དགའ་ལེགས་པའི་རྣམ་ཐར་རྒྱ་མཚོའི་སྙིང་པོ་མཐོང་བ་དོན་ལྡན་).

translated into English by Keith Dowman in the book *The Divine Madman: The Sublime Life and Songs of Drukpa Kunley*. This book, containing sacred tales of Drukpa Kunley by Needrup Zangpo, continues this tradition by adding another Bhutanese account of Drukpa Kunley to the list, but it stands out in bringing the stories of Drukpa Kunley written directly in English with some literary licence rather than directly translating existing books.

As the reader will see, in these highly embellished Bhutanese legends, Drukpa Kunley roams the region carrying a bow and arrows and wielding a phallus, the 'flaming thunderbolt', with which he subjugated many demons. He is also represented in art wearing a yogic dress rather than monastic robes and accompanied by a dog, bow and arrows, and sometimes a lady by his side. The Bhutanese depict Drukpa Kunley not only as an enlightened saint but as a master of magical power, who used miracles to convert those he encountered to spirituality and religion. In their accounts, we find a recurring theme of his subjugation of non-human forces in the form of demons and spirits, just like the legends of Padmasambhava's taming of malevolent spirits across the Himalayan world.

There are also many accounts of Drukpa Kunley performing miracles and spiritual feats to liberate the faithful from suffering and the cycle of rebirth. There are stories about how, on his first trip to Bhutan, he liberated a lady in north Paro by shooting an arrow through her armpit, liberated another by making her corpse walk to the funeral pyre and how he helped two elderly devotees attain a 'rainbow body'—a particular mode of full enlightenment—by chanting obscene prayers. Today, Bhutanese believers take these accounts of miracles and the use of magical power literally and consider Drukpa Kunley's outrageous deeds as sublime and skilful acts of a buddha. They are not to be construed as ordinary acts of debauchery and violence, which anyone can emulate. However, his autobiography, which records his first trip to Bhutan in order to visit Taktshang—or what is today known as the Tiger's Nest Temple—does not recount such works of miracle, but mentions him enjoying food, alcohol and archery, and exhorting locals to avoid disturbing beehives or killing lice. It records a powerful spiritual conversation he had with the Kathogpa lama at Taktshang on spirituality and material enjoyments.

In addition to recounting his spiritual prowess to tame unruly beings, liberate the faithful, turn crops into phalluses, urinate liquid gold, fold a knife into a knot, bring back dead animals to life, and so on, later accounts also present him as a lively, frolicking, carefree, comical character who had a jovial and lewd lifestyle, travelling from place to place enjoying local liquor, singing licentious songs and seducing women. Drukpa Kunley is said to have been a handsome and well-endowed priest who could charm any girl. Sex and alcohol were used as means for building spiritual connections and catalysts for speeding up the process of enlightenment. Bawdy songs and jokes were used to undo the fetters of social inhibitions and cultural taboos.

In the true fashion of a crazy-wisdom master, he is said to have used uninhibited and provocative methods to free people from ordinary perceptions, prejudices, conventions and sociocultural constrictions. Through his humorous and satirical songs and behaviour, he attacked the hypocrisy, corruption and self-aggrandizement of established institutions. The Bhutanese stories of his life are full of humour, mischief and mockery of orthodoxy, but these acts were clearly intended to convey a deeper message and purpose. His character, according to these accounts, epitomizes at once both frivolity of conduct and seriousness of religious purpose. That is roughly the persona of Drukpa Kunley perpetuated in the Bhutanese imagination today.

The historical person, as presented in his original writings, may have been less colourful and more sober. He was definitely a very learned scholar and an unparalleled critic of the corrupt and hypocritical elements of Tibetan Buddhist practices. He was an itinerant traveller and an inspiring poet. Above all, he was a spiritual figure who genuinely saw through ritualistic and materialistic trappings. Yet, it is the lively, humorous and satirical side of Drukpa Kunley's personality and his role as a miracle man that appeal most to the sensibility of his Bhutanese followers and that they remember best. Such accounts of miracles and his whimsical character may have initially spread even during Drukpa Kunley's lifetime, but they surely got exaggerated and embellished as the stories spread orally from valley to valley after his days.

In our attempts to unpack the complex and paradoxical depiction of Drukpa Kunley, it is worth noting that the fantastic Bhutanese stories of Drukpa Kunley were not merely fictitious creations for entertainment or edification produced through a conscious and deliberate flight of imagination. The Bhutanese accounts, which would be seen as mythical and legend-laden from a secular point of view, spring from a perspective in which the world is replete with invisible forces of nature and in which the power of mind transcends the constraints imposed by the ordinary sense of space and time. In recounting the tales of spirits and miracles, the Bhutanese authors were not merely deploying magical realism in their stories. To them, the existence of spirits and deities and Drukpa Kunley's miracles were as real as the food they ate. Even today, the traditional Bhutanese lives a deeply spiritual life steeped in belief in things that some others may consider mythical.

Primarily, there is the ancient pre-Buddhist animistic belief system, which informs the Bhutanese view of the natural surroundings. Mountains are seen as abodes of mountain deities, cliffs as residences of powerful rock spirits, forests as haunts of gods and demons, water bodies as residences of water spirits, etc. The world is teeming with invisible spirits who share the same habitat with visible lifeforms. The spread of Buddhism since the eighth century added another layer to the Bhutanese cultural make-up. As a science of the mind and art of mind training, Buddhism underscored the centrality of the mind/spirit in sentient existence. It did not eliminate the belief in the forces of nature but supplemented it with the belief in the inner potential and power of the mind, especially when it is fully transformed or enlightened. When fully harnessed, the power of the human mind or psyche can surpass the power of matter. Thus, Drukpa Kunley's miracles are seen as simply instances of exercising the mind's power over matter, time and space. An enlightened and liberated mind can transcend the ordinary notions of materiality, temporality and positionality.

This view, in turn, is grounded in the sophisticated Buddhist philosophical thought in which all phenomena are seen as illusory and inherently empty of real nature. Buddhist philosophers hold the view that all phenomena lack an absolute reality. There is no such thing as an absolute fact; there are only multiple conventional truths perceived from different perspectives. The empirical world is a fluid and dynamic experience processed through diverse sociocultural conditioning and perspectives. There is no ultimate point for fixation: truth and falsity are empty and artificial categories. Such philosophical thinking removes any rigid temporal and spatial strictures. Time, space, mind and matter are viewed as dynamic expressions of innate energy, which an enlightened mind such as Drukpa Kunley's can easily alter and change.

Bhutanese narrators of the supernatural acts of Drukpa Kunley view his life from such a philosophical point of view, which allows them to cohesively accommodate the magical elements. Thus, it is with such *emic* understanding of the cultural context that we can and indeed must appreciate the fanciful accounts and their significance for the intended audience. It is important for us to be aware of the spatio-temporal background from which the stories have emerged in order to properly understand their purpose and effect, and not see them from an *etic* perspective and dismiss them as unfounded naïve beliefs.

The same can be said for the Bhutanese depiction and admiration of Drukpa Kunley's maverick behaviour and indulgence in sex and alcohol. Like most pre-industrial primitive societies, traditional Bhutan revelled in the consumption of alcohol and often indulged in sexual laxity and promiscuity. People were more relaxed and open, especially before the spread of religious morality and modern puritanical sensibilities. Similarly, the phallus was a widespread symbol of fertility long before Drukpa Kunley's arrival in Bhutan. The role of sex and alcohol in the tantric form of Buddhism, which Tibet and Bhutan received from India, further reinforced such an outlook and attitude. Bhutanese devotees were used to hearing stories of debauchery, alcohol consumption and scandalous behaviour in the life of the tantric savants, particularly of the mahasiddhas, long before the appearance of Drukpa Kunley. In their eyes, Drukpa Kunley was only living up to the sublime ideals and high spiritual standards of the hermits and wisdom masters of yore.

Yet, the stories of Drukpa Kunley stand out to the Bhutanese because they look up to him with a deep sense of affection and pride as one of their own, at least in terms of religious affiliation. Although there were numerous Buddhist figures who performed miracles and practised crazy wisdom, Drukpa Kunley was one figure who was closely associated with Bhutan. Thus, we can understand the Bhutanese enthusiasm in telling and retelling his stories, as is the case with this new rendition in English.

Apart from a family line which continued for a few generations after him and a few sites loosely associated with him, Drukpa Kunley has hardly left any legacy in terms of institutional establishments or religious doctrine or practices. Yet, his influence on the Bhutanese religious and cultural consciousness is far-reaching. For one, the figure of Drukpa Kunley can be given much credit—though not all—for the libertine sexual character of the traditional Bhutanese man and woman. As much as Bhutan provided a fertile ground for the diffusion of the wild stories of Drukpa Kunley, the stories, in a process of circular reinforcement, bolstered the traditional unrestrained attitude and ubiquity of sexual symbols. The same can be said about the Bhutanese indulgence in alcohol, and the easy-going attitude to life and the robust sense of humour that are found abundantly in traditional Bhutanese society.

However, there are a few very important influences the stories of Drukpa Kunley had, and should continue to have, on Bhutan and the rest of the world, for that matter. A fundamental and overarching message contained in the stories of Drukpa Kunley is the Buddhist focus on the inner mind or spirit. In the Buddhist system, happiness is essentially a state of the mind, and material prosperity without spiritual well-being is meaningless. A true sense of fulfilment and meaning in life can only be attained through the proper development of the inner spirit by harnessing its full potential—the innate buddha nature. Today, as materialism sweeps across the globe fuelled by relentless commercial greed, places like traditional Bhutan where due attention is given to the inner development of the mind are rare to come by. Even in Bhutan, rising materialism is beginning to erode the traditional spiritual culture of being *nangpa,* or insiders who give priority to inner transformation and well-being over external things. As the human mind gets ever more neglected, stressed and restless in this fast-paced digital world, there is an urgent need to promote this tradition.

Another cultural ethos prevalent in the stories of Drukpa Kunley is the traditional view of the natural environment in which human beings and other forms of life must coexist in harmony. Sadly, the opposite outlook of anthropocentricity and human domination of other forms of life is rampant in most parts of the world, leaving a severe impact on biodiversity and the health of the planet. In these times, faced with the unprecedented challenges of climate change and environmental degradation, there is a critical need to cultivate respect for the non-human world comprising both visible and invisible life forms.

Finally, a very striking element in Drukpa Kunley's stories and writings is the culture of critical thinking. Both in the stories of his life and in his own writings, Drukpa Kunley can be seen as a sharp and scathing critic of institutional hypocrisies and corruption. As cultures age and institutions grow in wealth and power, they become stagnated and dysfunctional and often lose their original purpose and principles. Religious institutions and cultural traditions in particular face such stagnation and remain trapped in hierarchical structures, hollow rituals and mindless customs. The stories of Drukpa Kunley remind us to question our habitual tendencies, the self-same institutional structures and cultural traditions, so that we do not end up as people without principles, religion without spiritual efficacy and a society without social conscience.

These timeless intangible values and outlooks, embedded in the life and writings of Drukpa Kunley, shall remain as the most enduring and precious legacies of the mad master. This book by Needrup Zangpo no doubt will help sustain and spread them.

Preface

Not long after he renounced monastic life, Drukpa Kunley[1], the fearless maverick, burst into the marketplace of Lhasa, the capital of Tibet, bustling with people from across the Himalayan region. He shouted, addressing the milling crowd, 'Listen up, folks! I am Drukpa Kunley from Ralung. I have come here for the well-being of sentient beings. Please tell me where in your country can I find good chang[2] and beautiful girls?'

Someone from the crowd asked why he was inquiring about good chang and beautiful girls instead of virtuous lamas and peaceful monasteries if he had come to Lhasa for the well-being of sentient beings. It was a contradiction for the multitude

---

1 He was known by various names, such as Drukpa Kunga Legpa, Druk Nyon Kunga Legpa (Drukpa Madman Kunga Legpa), Choje Kunga Legpa (Dharma Lord Kunga Legpa), Kunga Legpi Paljor Zangpo, Kunga Legpi Pal Zangpo, Tshewang Gyalpo, and sometimes Drukpa Nyonpa. In Bhutan, he is popularly known as Lama or Lam Drukpa Kunley. He liked to call himself Jatang Kunley (Carefree Kunley), Kunley, or simply Drukpa. In this book, he is referred to as Drukpa Kunley.

2 It is an umbrella term for alcoholic beverages. His biography by Je Gedun Rinchen also uses the word sumchang (གསུམ་ཆང་), an alcoholic beverage filtered from fermented grains, interchangeably with chang. Chang could also mean ara (ཨ་རག་), an alcoholic beverage distilled from fermented grains, which is popular in Bhutan.

XXV

accustomed to puritanical and prudish sociocultural conventions and mores. For them, chang and beautiful girls were antithetical to spiritual pursuit.

However, for Drukpa Kunley, teaching and practising the Buddha dharma was not confined to rigid, dogmatic principles and approaches. He had realized at an early age that dharma is, ultimately, in the mind and not in external manifestations and projections. Guarding one's mind, he declared, is tantamount to observing all moral vows. He is known to have asked: Without recognizing the buddha within, what use is the persistent search without?[3]

The people thronging the marketplace, including many Bhutanese traders and pilgrims, were appalled by Drukpa Kunley's bold and provocative inquiry. They were yet to recognize him as a yogi who had transcended sociocultural and institutional inhibitions and trappings.

Drukpa Kunley was someone for whom chang and girls were not necessarily detrimental to spiritual awakening. Instead, they were unconventional vehicles for his teachings. He had left behind the suffocating orthodoxy of Buddhism, which became the target of his scathing critiques. He chose to teach, reprimand, censure, satirize and expose (its) hypocrisy. However, that does not mean that he condoned chang and sex. In fact, he warned religious practitioners against them.

Drukpa Kunley condemned the widespread religious hypocrisy in monastic establishments as disgraceful and reprehensible. He condemned hypocrisy as a canker eating away at the quintessence of the Buddha dharma. He saw the deep-rooted hypocrisy in the ostentatious cultural and moralistic paraphernalia of monastic

---

3 པདམ་རྒྱས་རང་ལ་ཡོད་པ་མ་ཤེས་ན། ། བྱེད་ཀྱིས་ནོར་འཚོལ་འདི་འདྲས་ཅི་བྱུང་པ། །

establishments. He also saw it in religious figures whose speech and behaviour were inconsistent with Buddhist values. Critique of hypocrisy is the single biggest theme running through Drukpa Kunley's songs, poems and conversations.

Any behaviour without hypocrisy, he said, can be an object of veneration[4]. He asserted that leading an unpretentious, ordinary life is far more honourable than a scholarly, religious life rife with duplicity. He took particular pride in his authenticity, often emphasizing it amidst self-deprecating remarks and as one of his spiritual commitments.

Drukpa Kunley became a fierce non-conformist because he did not want to be a part of the religious community that practised dharma for mere biological sustenance. He declared, 'I don't teach not because I don't want to teach, or because I can't teach, or because there are no listeners. I don't teach because all teachers today teach only for food and clothing.' He said that dharma teachers of his time 'do not even have a whiff of the dharma'[5]. He described them as 'lay people in yellow robes'[6].

Therefore, he became, in his own words, an aimless wandering yogi[7] employing alcohol, sex and antinomic behaviour to show the way and teach people. This is how Drukpa Kunley described himself: 'Happiness moves me to tears, and comfort makes me carefree. Meeting people feels meaningless, yet I yearn for company when I'm alone. When I want to stay, I leave. When I want to go, I remain. I listen to no one and get along with no one.'

---

4 ཀུན་འཛོམས་མེད་ནུ་སྤྱོད་པ་ཐམས་ཅད་ཕྱག་འཚལ་ལོ།

5 ཆོས་ཀྱི་དྲི་མེད།

6 སྐྱ་བོ་སེར་གཟུགས་པ།

7 ཕྱོགས་མེད་རྒྱལ་ཁམས་བསྐོར་བའི་རྣལ་འབྱོར་པ།

He wandered as a mendicant free and fearless of worldly concerns and monastic conventions. He said being attached to a monastic institution or community brought endless expectations and fostered a sense of permanence, both of which hindered spiritual growth. However, neither were his wanderings aimless nor alcohol, sex and crazy behaviour a sign of debauched morality. He saw both good and bad as part of one existence as he had transcended dualistic tendencies and perceptions.

Drukpa Kunley provided penetrating insights into the triviality of human habits and mindsets, powerfully illustrating lofty concepts like detachment, impermanence and dependent origination[8] through spontaneous deeds. Every time a devotee offered him an item of clothing or a piece of jewellery, he would wear it briefly and give it back, remarking, 'I've worn it once. Nobody will wear it forever.' Through this deed, he taught the concept of detachment and impermanence without using religious jargon.

⁂

While in Paro, Lama Tshewang of Gangtakha hamlet invited Drukpa Kunley to consecrate his newly built house. 'May the

---

[8] It is a fundamental teaching that explains how all phenomena arise and cease due to interconnected causes and conditions. It is often summarized as 'because this exists, that exists; because this ceases, that ceases.' In short, dependent origination describes reality as a web of interdependent processes, where nothing exists independently or in isolation. It emphasizes that everything we experience, including our thoughts, feelings, and even our sense of identity, is conditioned by a network of interrelated causes. This teaching challenges the belief in a fixed or permanent essence, showing that everything is in constant flux and is subject to change based on the conditions.

house be blessed with plenty of people and plenty of corpses,' Drukpa Kunley prayed. He prayed for Lama Tshewang's family to flourish. But the family misunderstood him and said that the prayer was inauspicious. 'May this house be blessed with few people and few corpses,' Drukpa Kunley corrected himself to make the family happy. As a result, the family dwindled and disappeared.

According to another folk story, Drukpa Kunley came across a group of women transplanting paddy while he was in Punakha. 'What are you planting with your soft thighs bare and exposed?' he teased them. 'We are planting phalluses,' answered the women in jest. 'May your phalluses grow well,' said Drukpa Kunley. That season, all the paddy saplings these women transplanted grew into a strange phallus-shaped weeds.

Through these deeds in Paro and Punakha, he underlined how the principle of dependent origination affects all actions. In Bhutan, elders and parents say we should be careful what we say and do in important and potent moments in life, for it will affect the future course of action.

※

Drukpa Kunley left behind not only a distinguished lineage that continues to this day, but also an enduring legacy that pervades the country's history, literature, folklore and public psyche. The eighth reincarnation and great-grandson of Gyalse Tenzin Rabgay (1638-1696), Gyalse Chogtrul Jigme Tenzin Wangpo (b. 1993), has kept his illustrious lineage alive after almost five hundred years. Drukpa Kunley may not have left behind institutional legacies, but he is among the best-loved Tibetan saints who visited Bhutan. He is the most prominent figure in

Bhutan's historical and cultural imagination. The mere mention of his name brings smiles to the faces of the Bhutanese.

Drukpa Kunley visited Bhutan many times and travelled throughout the country. Among towering Bhutanese figures, he met Terton Pema Lingpa (1450-1521) several times. They enjoyed each other's company and developed mutual admiration and respect.

Drukpa Kunley seems to have visited Bhutan even in his old age. While he was in Gon, present-day Gasa, with Lama Ngawang Chogyal (1465-1540)[9], he said he would return to Ralung like an old bird to its roost, tired of ceaseless roaming.

Drukpa Kunley (1455-1529) was among the earliest Drukpa Kagyu masters to visit Bhutan. He is one of the three holy madmen of Tibet who lived during the fifteenth and sixteenth centuries, the other two being Tsang Nyon Heruka[10] or the Madman of Tsang (1452-1507) and Ü Nyon Kunga Zangpo or the Madman of Ü (1458-1532).

Drukpa Kunley was born into a collateral line of the illustrious Drukpa family of Ralung. He is believed to be the reincarnation

---

9 Ngawang Chogyal, also known as Ngawang Choje or Drukchen Ngawang Chogyal, is believed to be Drukpa Kunley's younger brother, cousin, or nephew. Mipham Tshewang Tenzin's biography of Drukpa Kunley identifies Ngawang Chogyal as Drukpa Kunley's elder brother. In this book, he is identified as Drukpa Kunley's cousin. At one point in Drukpa Kunley's life, he was the abbot of Ralung Monastery. Ngawang Chogyal was the great-great-grandfather of Zhabdrung Ngawang Namgyal, the founding father of the Bhutanese state.

10 Tsang Nyon Heruka is widely known for his authorship of the authoritative biography and songs of Milarepa.

of two Indian adepts, Saraha[11] and his disciple Shavaripa[12]. His approach to both practising and teaching the dharma was similar to that of these adepts—devoid of ritualism and scholasticism. Drukpa Kunley is depicted like them in iconographic paintings. Saraha is depicted holding an arrow while Shavaripa is depicted holding a bow and an arrow. Drukpa Kunley is depicted singing, or holding his bow, quiver, or lute.

Drukpa Kunley experienced a traumatic childhood. His father was murdered in a family feud, which disillusioned him to become a monk at the age of seven. Nothing out of the ordinary seems to have happened in the next eighteen years of his life as a monk. He was believed to have become a spiritual adept at the age of twenty-five. That is when he decided to leave the monastery and dissociate himself from all institutional bondages of the dharma. And that is when he came to be known as Divine Madman Drukpa Kunley.

However, Drukpa Kunley was anything but mad. He was a realized master who found the mundane world utterly vain, hypocritical, and insane. He dismissed what the rest of the world pursued with grave seriousness as trivial and ludicrous. He and the mundane world were at two extremes of the spiritual spectrum. They found each other to be mad. Drukpa Kunley was undeniably highly eccentric. But there is discipline and elegance in his eccentricity and insanity. He was not an indolent vagrant aimlessly wandering in search of free food, drinks and sex.

---

11 Saraha was one of the greatest Indian adepts and is known as the arrow maker. He was one of Nagarjuna's teachers.

12 Shavaripa was one of the eighty-four adepts of India. He was a hunter who became a disciple of Nagarjuna and a teacher of Maitripa. Shavaripa is a key figure in the transmission of the early Mahamudra lineage of teachings in India.

His time with Palzang Buthri, his consort from Lhasa, gives us a glimpse into his daily routine. His day was divided into four quarters. From dawn to noon, he relished his chang. From noon to sundown, he delighted in making music. From dusk to midnight, he made love to Palzang Buthri. And from midnight to dawn, he meditated on the essence of Mahamudra[13]. So, despite what random touristic writings on him would have us believe, his days were not misspent on chang, sex, and heterodox behaviour; he actually used them as unconventional vehicles for teaching and awakening.

In fact, he dismissed unwise behaviour that did not correspond with duezhi[14] or the four quarters of the day. He repudiated madness that made no sense. There was a method to his madness because he was adept at both divine and worldly doctrines[15].

Having said that, it is important to note that Drukpa Kunley is far too complex and profound to be put into a neat category of practitioners. Although he is a historical figure, it is difficult to separate facts from fiction when it comes to his life. Therefore, putting his life under scholarly scrutiny and questioning the historicity of his deeds at face value may lead to losing the intrinsic appeal and value of his stories. Reading his stories with an open mind is critical to appreciating them.

---

13 Literally the 'great seal', the most direct practice for realizing buddha nature.

14 Morning, evening, day, night (ནུབ་ ཉིན་ མཚན་)
    སྔུད་པ་དུས་ཚོད་བཞི་དུས་མ་འགྱུར་ན། སྐྱེན་སྐྱོད་ཚུལ་པར་ས་འདི་ཚོས་སུ་ཡིན་པ།

15 ལྷ་ཆོས་མི་ཆོས་གཉིས་ཀ་ལ་ཕྱིན་ཏུ་མཁས་པ།

|| PREFACE || XXXIII

Most stories, references and allusions in this book have been drawn from these sources: the secret[16] biography of Drukpa Kunley by Gendün Rinchen, the sixty-ninth Je Khenpo[17] of Bhutan, titled *The Essence of a Sea of Biography of Drukpa Kunley That is Meaningful to Behold*[18]; *Biography of Drukpa Kunley Including His Deeds in Mon Paro*[19] by Mipham Tshewang Tenzin, the grandson of Drukpa Kunley—this is often referred to as an autobiography because it is written in the first person and believed to have been dictated by Drukpa Kunley himself; the four-volume autobiography (Ka, Kha, Ga, Nga) of Drukpa Kunley titled *Autobiography of Great Yogi Kunga Legpa*[20], and *Deeds of Lam Drukpa Kunley*[21] in Dzongkha, the national language of Bhutan—published by KMT Publishing House in Thimphu—which also captures popular oral stories and folktales about the yogi.

The translation of volume Ka of Drukpa Kunley's autobiography titled *More than a Madman: The Divine Words of Drukpa Kunley* by Elizabeth Monson and Chorten Tshering is a significant addition to access Drukpa Kunley's stories in English. *Tales of a Mad Yogi: The Life and Wild Wisdom of Drukpa Kunley* by Elizabeth Monson

---

16 Biographical writings about Buddhist masters fall into three categories—outer, inner, and secret. Secret biographies describe a master's meditative experiences, visions, and miraculous deeds, often inconceivable for ordinary people.

17 Chief Abbot of the Central Monastic Body of Bhutan.

18 འབྲུག་པ་ཀུན་ལེགས་ཀྱི་རྣམ་ཐར་རྒྱ་མཚོའི་སྙིང་པོ་མཐོང་བ་དོན་ལྡན།

19 འབྲུག་པ་ཀུན་ལེགས་ཀྱི་རྣམ་ཐར་མོན་སྤ་རོ་སོགས་ཀྱི་མཛད་སྤྱོད།

20 རྒྱལ་འབྱོར་གྱི་དབང་ཕྱུག་ཆེན་པོ་ཀུན་དགའ་ལེགས་པའི་རྣམ་ཐར།

21 བླམ་འབྲུག་པ་ཀུན་ལེགས་ཀྱི་མཛད་རྣམ།

retells many stories from his namthars[22], combining academic and creative approaches. The biographies of Drukpa Kunley tell the story of his life quite differently.

All the stories in this collection are based on the above Choekey—the classical Tibetan or dharma language—and Dzongkha sources and slightly different versions of oral stories I have heard from Bhutanese from various walks of life. Geshe Gendün Rinchen's biography of Drukpa Kunley, first published in 1966 in Bhutan, is the primary source of most stories. His work is, undoubtedly, the most concise, colourful, and popular story of Drukpa Kunley's life in Choekey and through translation, in the form of *The Divine Madman: The Sublime Life and Songs of Drukpa Kunley* by Keith Dowman in English. Geshe Gendün Rinchen's work is, in his own words, a distillation of a scattered collection of writings, often too fragmented, disjointed, or vast to be easily understood and enjoyed. It contains many stories from Drukpa Kunley's four-volume autobiography, often retold with slight variations, along with some popular folktales about the yogi.

The grandiloquent and euphemistic use of words and expressions in Choekey in the hagiographic style and their literal translation in English, coupled with fantastical oral stories, have rendered Drukpa Kunley almost mythical. Therefore, I have deliberately used plain words and expressions—while not sounding banal and gross—to make him look more human and easier to relate to. For example, I have not used euphemistic words like 'thunderbolt' and 'lotus' to refer to penis and vagina.

Close attention has been paid to making the imagery and descriptions related to Drukpa Kunley's physical appearance,

---

[22] Literally 'completely liberated', it is a biography, autobiography, or hagiography.

dress and locales of the stories as faithful to the Choekey sources as possible. To achieve realistic descriptions of the places in the stories, I have visited as many of them in Bhutan as possible. All the places can be located, but most characters cannot be located in history. Similarly, the artworks in this book are the closest we can come to recreating an image of Drukpa Kunley.

The namthars sufficiently establish that Drukpa Kunley was strikingly—some even say irresistibly—good-looking, well-endowed and had a pleasant voice. He was a cross between a layman and a religious person. People often mistook him for a beggar because his dress was limited to a dorgong, an upper garment shaped like a vajra that covers the shoulders, chest and upper back, and an angdar, a lower garment that covers the waist and thighs. But as Kongpo's Sumchogma, a girl he liberated, put it, even naked, he looked majestic and brilliant[23]; and within his completely ordinary body resided the mind of a Buddha[24].

The real Drukpa Kunley may not have been as colourful and flamboyant as his biographies portray him, because he is a much sober person in his autobiography. In the four-volume autobiography, we find Drukpa Kunley as a free and open-minded Buddhist going on pilgrimages, begging alms, visiting monasteries, meeting lamas and receiving teachings from them, giving dharma discourses and singing philosophical songs. We sometimes find him even conservative in his view of the dharma.

Many writings in English describe Drukpa Kunley as a philanderer or a womanizer and his sexual relations with women as 'sexual exploits'. But his namthars tell quite a different story. His sexual relationships are limited to girls he picks and chooses

---

23 གཅེར་བུའི་ཁྱམས་ལ་གཟི་བྱི་མདངས་ཆེ།
24 ཐ་མལ་ཁྱམས་ལ་རྒྱལ་བའི་ཐུགས།

based on their potential for spiritual accomplishments rather than their looks or his whims. All girls who have sexual relationships with him are spiritually inclined, and most of them accomplish spiritual awakening. Some of them even attain the phenomenon known as the rainbow body, which is explained in the fifth story in this collection.

Contrary to the popular narrative that portrays him as a man of poor sexual discipline, Drukpa Kunley is known to have said that girls suitable for him are rare: *'the marketplace may be teeming with girls, but the vagina I desire is rare'*[25].

Besides, Drukpa Kunley repeatedly underlined that he saw girls as mothers: 'I, Drukpa Kunley from Ralung, think of a loving girl as a mother'[26]. He cautioned the Seventh Karmapa Chodrak Gyatsho (1454–1506) that he must not be swayed by beautiful girls if he does not have this pure perception, which is at the heart of a bodhisattva's deeds.

Drukpa Kunley's encounter with the Karmapa makes for a delectable story with good humour, offers an insight into human nature, and an enduring moral lesson. The stories in this collection are all like this—delightful, compelling, and invigorating. Beyond stimulating thought and contemplation, Drukpa Kunley's stories have the potential to reignite our sense of humour that can make agitated modern life much more bearable. He underlines a sense of humour and a carefree attitude to life as essential elements in easing life's endless heartaches and tensions. He says, 'If my stories are filled with licentious talks, just take it easy,'[27] meaning do not stress yourself interpreting them through a moral lens.

---

25 བུ་མོ་ཁྲོམ་ཚོགས་གང་ལས་ཀྱང་། སྟུ་རང་ལ་མཁོ་བ་དཀོན་པོ་འདུག

26 ར་ལུང་གི་འབྲུག་པ་ཀུན་ལེགས་ང་། སྐྱིད་སྡུག་གི་བུ་མོ་ཨི་ཤོགས་སུ་མ་བཞིན་བསམ།

27 འཆལ་གཏམ་སྣ་ཚོགས་འདུག་ན་ཨ་ཅམས་དགའ་མཛོད།

Stories that dwell on weighty subjects and excessive eroticism have been consciously avoided. Stories that delve into complex philosophical and metaphysical concepts are too difficult for me to retell simply and clearly. Therefore, they might not be the best fit for the pleasurable literary reading experience that this collection aims to provide. To provide a smooth reading experience, I have used Choekey and Dzongkha words and expressions as sparingly as possible. For the same purpose, the use of footnotes has been kept to the minimum.

This anthology is a modest attempt to present parts of Drukpa Kunley's life in the modern idiom using creative non-fiction techniques. I have used a reasonable degree of creative licence to create scenes, incorporate dialogues and develop characters. I have interwoven biographical and oral stories wherever it made the stories more coherent and complete. Several oral stories from Bhutan and Tibet have been fully retold for the first time.

In addition to being largely inaccessible, Buddhist biographies and autobiographies written in Choekey can often prove difficult to read and enjoy as literary works. Therefore, this compilation is expected to enable English readers to read Drukpa Kunley's extraordinary life beyond the translation of terse and pithy Choekey. My aim is to make his stories more accessible and palatable to the modern reader. However, the anthology does not attempt to reconstruct a grand narrative that captures his life from birth to death. In fact, it does not capture many significant moments of his life.

Although the stories primarily involve creative retelling, they incorporate translations from Choekey, notably his songs and teachings in verse. While the translation tries to faithfully capture Choekey expressions and structures, it occasionally diverges from the direct meanings. These variations are deliberately employed to achieve poetic effects according to the English literary tradition.

To authentically portray Drukpa Kunley's persona, I have meticulously maintained the distinctive tone of his namthars throughout the narratives. This tone exudes an unbridled and liberating quality, particularly in its treatment of sexual themes and bold critiques of socio-cultural and religious norms. Drukpa Kunley's voice is unpredictably contemplative, sensitive, self-deprecating, skeptical, or even bawdy from moment to moment. Recognizing the sensibilities of contemporary readers, certain lines expressing extreme views on sexuality and gender have been thoughtfully moderated or omitted.

The stories do not follow a clear chronological sequence because we cannot find a distinct narrative structure in the namthars. However, a few stories from Bhutan and Tibet are arranged in some logical sequence. Every story in the anthology is a self-contained narrative that can be read independently of the others.

To give the book a sense of beginning and ending, it starts with the story of Drukpa Kunley shooting his arrow from Tibet, which brings him to Bhutan, and ends with his time in Gon, which appears to be his penultimate year in Bhutan.

The thirty-three stories presented here are brief episodes from the grand narrative. These episodes can be a good alternative for those who find the grand narrative too vast and profound to follow.

Needrup Zangpo
Thimphu, Bhutan

Prologue

All the lesser ascetic doctrines signify nothing
If they deviate from the words of the Buddha.
Self-fashioned wisdom is bereft of purpose
Without the blessings of an accomplished master.
What is the worth of all the reverential rituals
If we do not embrace all beings like our own children?
If we miss the very essence of the Three Vows[28],
What is the point of keeping one while breaking another?
Without recognizing the Buddha within,
What use is the persistent search without?
Failing to realize the natural equipoise of meditation,
Chasing after discursive thoughts is futile.
If conduct is not consistent with four quarters of the day,
Wild, befuddled lunacy is pointless.
Without realizing that there is no graspable view,
There is no use trying to find it among prejudiced notions.
Lust for sustenance without discipline and realization
Sows debts that need to be settled in future lives.
Wearing scanty clothing sans comfort and warmth,
What is the point of bearing the cold hell here and now?
Industry and labour without pith instructions is futile;
It is akin to ants clambering up a sand dune.

---

28 Three levels of ordination

Amassing knowledge without meditating on the nature of the mind
Is like starving oneself on the lap of riches.
A learned master who does not teach nor write serves no purpose
Just like a jewel on the head of a venomous snake.
A fool who teaches without anything to teach
Is simply proclaiming his ignorance far and wide.
Recognize and practise the essence of all teachings.

Translated from Geshe Gendün Rinchen's *The Essence of a Sea of Biography of Drukpa Kunley that is Meaningful to Behold* (འབྲུག་པ་ཀུན་ལེགས་ཀྱི་རྣམ་ཐར་རྒྱ་མཚོའི་སྙིང་པོ་མཐོང་བ་དོན་ལྡན་). The lines he spoke when he abandoned the monastic life succinctly encapsulate Drukpa Kunley's quintessential teachings.

CHAPTER 1

The Flight of the Messenger Arrow

It was a crisp, bright winter morning in the Nangkatse village of Tibet's Yamdro province. The warm rays of the sun had drawn the children out of their homes. All was quiet as usual when suddenly a thunderous sound tore through the air.

Startled, all the village elders rushed out, some with their breakfast bowls in hand, wondering how a bolt of thunder had struck the region on a brilliantly sunny day. They looked into the cloudless sky with quiet wonder as the thunderous sound faded into the south.

The children playing outside had seen what was happening. They said a certain lama had shot an arrow into the southern sky. 'Now fly to the house of a maiden destined to meet with me,' the lama had said before launching the arrow.

The lama was Drukpa Kunley. While sleeping in Lady Semzangma's house the previous night, he had had a dream. A dark-complexioned girl, clad in a yellow lower wrap-around and wielding a blazing ritual dagger, had appeared to him and had given a prophecy. 'Drukpa Kunley,' she said, 'your destiny lies in Lhomon[29] where you will propagate the dharma and serve all sentient beings. The time is now. In Lhomon, you will establish a lineage that will benefit the Drukpa Kagyu tradition in the future. At sunrise tomorrow, shoot an arrow to the south as a messenger.'

As the girl disappeared, Drukpa Kunley awoke to a breaking dawn. He knew that the girl was deity Palden Lhamo inviting him to Lhomon.

Palden Lhamo is one of the principal Drukpa Kagyu dharma protectors. In wrathful iconographic representation, she is dark

---

29 Bhutan's old name, meaning Southern Mon. Mon is a derivative of the Tibetan word *mun*, which means darkness. Bhutan was then known as Lhomon, or the southern land of darkness, because it was devoid of the light of Buddhism.

blue in colour, hence her dark complexion. She rides a mule across a sea of blood. She wears a skull crown and holds a skull cup filled with blood.

༶

The arrow soared high over the Himalayas. It glided over Bhutanese territory, followed a steady downward trajectory and roared over the mountains towards the village of Toep Lungdram Wogma in Punakha. As it soared low over the mountain towering over Danglo village in Wang, present-day Thimphu, its notch brushed against the crest of the mountain and left behind a huge dent that made the mountaintop look like the notch of an arrow. Today, the place is known as Datong Gonpa or the Arrow Notch Monastery.

The arrow descended towards its destination and tore through the crown of a mountain between Dochula and Hinglila, leaving behind a distinctive V-shaped groove in the mountaintop.

༶

Nestled securely within a narrow valley, Toep Lungdram Wogma was cradled by terraced paddy fields gently ascending the slope. The lush fields bordered low hills cloaked in subtropical vegetation. The village was a harmonious blend of tranquillity and abundance. Today, the village is known as Toep Chandana, meaning the village where the arrow landed.

A thunderous sound suddenly filled the peaceful village, making everybody working in the fields look around in shock. In seconds, as the thunderous sound hit a deafening pitch, something rocked the three-storey house of Toep Tshewang, a wealthy young man of considerable repute.

It was midday. Toep Tshewang's beautiful wife, Rigden Norbu Dzoma, was preparing to take the dishes to the nearby stream for washing after lunch. She dashed to the doorstep suspecting an earthquake when she saw, to her fright, a shuddering arrow firmly stuck on the wooden ladder with eleven steps.

The deeply religious Toep Tshewang comforted his wife and interpreted the strange arrow as a harbinger of a child for them. He tried to pull out the arrow with all his might but to no avail. No one else from the village could pull it out. However, when his wife pulled it, it came off easily like a strand of hair from a lump of butter. The ever-optimistic wife washed her hands, wrapped the arrow in a silk scarf, and reverently enshrined it in the altar.

In the meanwhile, Drukpa Kunley began his journey to Lhomon, following his arrow. As he headed south from the Tibetan town of Phari, his mind wandered back to a conversation he had had in Lhasa years back with an elderly woman from Lhomon. When he inquired where he would find good chang and beautiful girls, she had assured him that Lhomon had the finest of both. 'I shall come around to drink the southern chang and meet southern belles,' he had told her.

Drukpa Kunley crossed the Tremola Pass and traversed perilous mountains. As he crossed over to the Bhutanese side of the Himalaya, he came across nomadic communities. Black yak hair tents dotted wide meadows. He walked past sparkling emerald glacial lakes and frequently paused to admire their pristine beauty. He briefly stopped by the bank of one such lake. He dipped a finger into the lake and sprinkled a few drops of water into the air as a gesture of offering to all buddhas, bodhisattvas and local deities. Then he cupped his hands and drank deep from the lake. As he swallowed the ice-cold water, his throat constricted momentarily. He could feel every mouthful coursing down into his stomach, filling him with a refreshing and cooling sensation. To fully immerse himself in the experience, he closed his eyes, transforming the act into a meditative moment.

As he approached the nomadic communities of Soe and Naro, he spotted a flock of blue sheep grazing on a rocky cliffside. A herd of yaks grazed peacefully by a small stream that gurgled its way across a meadow sprinkled with colourful flowers. After crossing Soe and Naro, he came across a few Bhutanese traders and spent a night with them in the cave of Wodod Drak. Then, he journeyed through the villages of Paro, including Shingkarab, Sharna, Chuyur, and Drukgyal, ultimately arriving in Jagarthang.

From Paro, he crossed into the territory of Wang, where he subdued the demon of Gonsakha. While in Wang, he instinctively knew that his arrow had flown beyond Dochula, the mountain pass between Wang and Wangdi. So, he followed the old footpath between Wang and Wangdi and headed straight to Toep Lungdram Wogma.

Outside Toep Tshewang's house, he pulled down his angdar and urinated by the footpath. A group of children walked past him, but he did not bother to pull up his angdar. 'Your genitals are unusually long and dangling,' they said to him, giggling. 'This is the season of long and dangling genitals,' he said, smiling.

Walking into Toep Tshewang's house, he inquired, 'My arrow has come this way. Has it arrived here?'

Toep Tshewang greeted him warmly and said, 'An arrow has landed here. Does it belong to you? Please sit down.'

As Drukpa Kunley was about to sit, Rigden Norbu Dzoma appeared before him like a spring bloom. She was fair, slender and graceful. Her face was like a fresh blossom on which her dark eyes hovered like bees. Her lips were like supple petals of a coral flower. Her dark hair was long enough to cover part of her cheeks aglow with a subtle hint of red.

'My arrow has found its mark in the abode of this angelic beauty,' he declared. 'Step aside, host Tshewang. I need your wife.' He pulled her towards him and gathered her in his embrace.

Aghast and seething with fury, Toep Tshewang unsheathed a sword and confronted Drukpa Kunley. 'Even before exchanging pleasantries and warming your seat, you make advances on the hostess! This may be tolerated in Tibet, but this is an unheard-of atrocity here.'

Throwing his right hand around Rigden Norbu Dzoma's neck, Drukpa Kunley deftly snatched the sword with the left and twisted the sword into a tight knot. Toep Tshewang was awestruck. He submitted himself to Drukpa Kunley and said, 'I didn't know that you are a buddha. You may take my wife. Please stay here as my lama for the rest of my life.' This incident gave rise to this popular expression:

> Toepa Tshewang loves the dharma,
> Carefree Kunley loves the hostess,
> May the dharma lover and hostess lover bring good luck.[30]

Drukpa Kunley agreed to stay in Toep Lungdram Wogma for some time. During his sojourn there, he subdued the demon of the upper reaches of the valley and sealed it in a boulder. The demon could be heard pleading from inside the boulder, 'Drukpa Kunley, let me go back to Lungdram Wogma.'

---

30 སྟོད་པ་ཚེ་དབང་ཆོས་ལ་དགའ། བྱ་བྲལ་ཀུན་དགའ་ཡུལ་གསས་མོ་དགའ། ཆོས་དགའ་གསས་དགའ་བདེ་ལེགས་ཤོག

While he was there, his son Ngawang Tenzin[31], the progenitor of his lineage, was born to Rigden Norbu Dzoma. Ngawang Tenzin's son was Tshewang Tenzin, who would become an important patron of the dharma in Bhutan. When Zhabdrung Ngawang Namgyal, his relative, came to Bhutan in 1616, Tshewang Tenzin became his principal host and patron. He offered Tango Monastery to Zhabdrung and oversaw the construction of Cheri Monastery where Zhabdrung instituted Bhutan's first monastic order with thirty monks.

Ngawang Tenzin's grandson and Tshewang Tenzin's son, Gyalse Tenzin Rabgay, became an important disciple of Zhabdrung Ngawang Namgyal and the Fourth Druk Desi or the temporal ruler of Bhutan. Although Drukpa Kunley's family line in Bhutan ended with Gyalse Tenzin Rabgay, it continued through the line of his incarnations. The eighth reincarnation of Gyalse Tenzin Rabgay, Gyalse Chogtrul Jigme Tenzin Wangpo, is today the chief abbot of Tango University of Buddhist Studies, the highest Drukpa Kagyu seat of learning in Bhutan.

Deity Palden Lhamo's prophecy given to Drukpa Kunley in Nangkatse in the fifteenth century stays relevant to this day. The messenger arrow had found its mark.

---

31 Ngawang Tenzin was believed to be the reincarnation of Sangdag Garton, one of the five sons of Phajo Drukgom Zhigpa, who was among the first Drukpa lamas to visit Bhutan from Tibet.

CHAPTER 2

An Egg-headed Beast to the Rescue

AN EGG-HEADED BEAST TO THE RESCUE | 9

A group of travellers had just emptied a pot of churned butter tea and a bamboo container of puffed rice. They agreed that the quick snack should be good enough as dinner in a rugged wilderness inhabited by easily irritable spirits.

They were in the cave of Wodod Drak, a desolate rocky hillside sparsely covered by stunted oaks and alpine shrubs. A turbulent stream cascaded down the narrow gorge, its roar echoing through the craggy landscape. The place, as the Bhutanese would describe it, was wedged between the shadow of a cliff and the relentless rush of a river.

As the pot and bamboo container were put back into a cane basket, the sun sank behind the horizon. A small fire, fed by dry twigs, turned red as the last rays of the sun left the cave.

The travellers talked in hushed voices. One who kept the fire going snapped the twigs gingerly to avoid loud, cracking sounds. Another picked up his rosary and started chanting mani, the six-syllable mantra of Chenrezig, the bodhisattva of compassion. Another spread his bedding in the deepest corner of the cave. One of them stared at the disappearing sun with a forlorn expression.

No sooner had the sun completely disappeared behind the mountains than a sprightly man, a cross between a monk and a beggar, greeted the travellers boisterously. He wore long, uncombed hair and a pair of huge, round earrings.

'This is a rocky hillside not ideal for travellers to camp,' he declared as he barged into the cave. The bewildered travellers exchanged uneasy glances but remained silent.

The hillside of Wodod Drak between Phari in Tibet and Shingkarab in Lhomon was turning dark. The alpine shrubs dotting the rocky hillside looked increasingly like crawling ogres from Bhutanese folktales.

Still standing, the sprightly man continued to talk loudly about his coming from Tibet and going to Lhomon. The travellers became increasingly nervous and anxious. The malevolent demon of the place could be disturbed and infuriated.

'Can I camp here with you tonight?' asked the wildly confident man. The travellers exchanged questioning glances. The oldest among them said in a soft and dismissive tone, 'Sleep there,' pointing to the mouth of the cave.

When silence returned to the cave after the newcomer settled down, the oldest traveller said in a deliberately loud voice before sleeping, 'May I be protected, Lord Demon of Wodod.' All of his companions echoed the supplication almost in unison, 'May I be protected, Lord Demon of Wodod.'

The Tibetan man said equally loudly, 'May I be protected, My Own Thing.'

The travellers looked at one another and winced.

Silence returned to the cave once again, broken only by the soft rustle of leaves, distant rumble of the stream, and the occasional hoot of an owl. Soon, the tired travellers drifted into peaceful slumber.

At around midnight, the demon of Wodod Drak, to whom all travellers paid obeisance, came stomping by, his hair violently cascading behind him. 'What special thing do you have that you must seek protection from?' he demanded of the Tibetan man in a guttural growl. This startled the travellers out of their sleep. They all sat up and huddled together in the deepest corner of the cave, petrified. They muttered incoherent bits of prayers.

The Tibetan man was not frightened. He took his time to sit up. He looked the ferocious demon straight in the eye and thrust out his rock-hard penis saying, 'I have this one'.

'Oho! What a strange beast this is!' exclaimed the demon. 'Its head is like an egg, its trunk is like a fish, and its root is like a pig.'

The travellers, frozen with fear, could not believe what was happening. One of them wondered what a strange thing it was to do to a ruthless demon. Another thought they were sure to pay with their lives for the Tibetan vagrant's foolishness. There was one among them with a more contemplative nature, who felt a mysterious power emanating from the Tibetan man's penis, which soothed his whole being paralysed with fear.

As the greatly perplexed demon stood before the man muttering to himself, 'This is a fish-bodied, egg-headed pig-like beast', the man sprang up and thrust his hard penis into its mouth, saying, 'If you don't know what it is, this is what it is.' The demon let out a sharp squeal like a pig struck unawares by an arrow and tumbled away with his front teeth smashed in. The hills echoed his squeal.

After a long while, a subdued-looking man walked up to the Tibetan man and knelt before him, his eyes downcast. He was shaking. Wodod Demon, in his peaceful manifestation, submitted himself to the Tibetan man and pledged that he would never harm any life thereafter.

The benumbed travellers discovered that the wildly confident man was Drukpa Kunley, the Holy Madman of Druk.

CHAPTER 3

The Demoness who Wears a Skin Dress

THE DEMONESS WHO WEARS A SKIN DRESS

In a dense forest of blue pine between Wodod Drak and Paro, a demoness was perpetually bogged down by the weight of her skin dress that she was forced to wear centuries ago.

In the summer, her dress got soaked in the rain and turned into an enormous mass, too heavy for her to lift. She wriggled, squirmed and twisted under the garment throughout the wet summer, starving and whimpering helplessly.

Come icy winter and the dress froze and bound her like a straitjacket. The frozen mass of hide clung to her so tightly that she was rendered immobile. Day and night, summer and winter, she was thus pinned to the same spot, perpetually starving. Every day, she could see a stream of travellers walk past her with their yaks and horses but nobody saw her or heard her piteous whimpers.

She had now lost sense of the hills of Shingkarab, once her sovereign domain. But the image of a rugged man armed with a bow and arrows still sat large on her mind.

It was a typical day at Shingkarab. The sun was a few metres above the eastern horizon. The ill-fated demoness had overslept and awoke to a gnawing hunger. She immediately prepared to survey her territory.

Paro-bound travellers, who had halted the previous night in the cave of Wodod Drak, would pass by her territory before the sun hit the zenith. Wary travellers often slipped past her home without making the faintest of sounds. She had cursed herself several times for letting them run past Shingkarab before she noticed them.

Today, she was particularly vigilant.

She emerged from her dwelling in her natural terrifying form. Her snarling maw and bulging, bloodshot eyes occupied a large portion of her face. Her long hair flowed down the back of her head and temples in tangled tresses. As she walked clumsily, she grunted with short laborious breaths. Her lips, parted by elongated, interlocking fangs were red and wet. Her digits bore long and thick nails resembling the talons of a predator.

She had hardly taken a few steps when she saw a lone figure gliding down the narrow path in the distance. 'A surefooted pilgrim from Lhomon, and all alone,' she thought, a satisfied sigh escaping her.

As the solitary figure drew nearer, she swiftly transformed into a beautiful girl and waited by the wayside.

'Where are you coming from?' enquired the girl as the traveller, equipped with a bow and arrows, approached. A sturdy hunting dog followed him. The man was scantily clad and wore a pair of rough leather sandals strapped to the ankles. His face was weather-beaten and his hair dishevelled, but he looked enchantingly happy and self-assured.

'I'm coming from Tibet,' replied the traveller, arms akimbo in a restful, rather than an arrogant way.

'So where do you live and where are you going?' enquired the traveller.

'I live in the mountains around here, and I've come here in search of food.'

'What do you eat and what do you wear?'

'I eat human flesh and wear human skin whenever I get one,' replied the girl, now unsmiling.

'Well then, wear this,' the traveller said, skinning his scrotums and miraculously covering the girl with it.

The demoness was left behind pleading and whimpering under the blanket of human skin as the traveller, Drukpa Kunley, resumed his journey towards Paro.

CHAPTER 4

Arresting the Sun's Descent to Build a Stupa

'Another, please,' he said. 'Your turnip is luscious.'

Drukpa Kunley had reached Sharna village in Paro from Tibet. He had stopped to talk to an old woman harvesting turnips by the footpath. Despite her diminutive stature, she had managed to pull out a few backloads of fat turnips. She was sweating profusely in the midday sun.

Drukpa Kunley had just devoured a huge turnip. The old woman graciously handed him another. He rubbed off the mud and munched on it furiously. Within seconds, he asked for another, and yet another. When he had gobbled up more than a backload of turnips, the old woman said she could not give away all her harvest to an outlandish passerby.

'Very well then,' said Drukpa Kunley, smiling. 'Thank me for all the turnips I've eaten for you.'

The old woman was taken aback. Before she could say anything, Drukpa Kunley strode out of sight. 'What a strange man,' she found herself saying aloud.

It was autumn in Paro. The landscape of Sharna had transformed into a rich tapestry of golds, oranges and reds, offering a striking contrast against the sacred white peaks towering above the village and the clear blue expanse of the sky overhead. Further down south, the fertile valleys of Paro were golden with ripening rice. It was time for the farmers to 'collect gold by the handful', as the Bhutanese describe the autumn season.

In the distance, a glacial stream funnelled through a narrow gorge, its waters churning into frothy cascades resembling billows of cotton floating on a bed of turquoise. The old woman hardly noticed the autumnal splendour surrounding her.

As the day waned, she wearily made her way home, carrying as many turnips as she could. Her two-storey house was a rich imitation of Sharna's autumnal spectacle with a burst of fiery hues. Its thick, mud-rammed walls were painted white, while its windows and wooden accents were adorned with a vibrant array of animal and floral motifs.

Imposing on either side, flanking the entrance, were two huge phalluses, their roots adorned with a thicket of hair, and their tip spewing a jet of frothy liquid. The phalluses, much bigger and taller than the old woman, symbolized fertility and protection against evil spirits.

As she opened the storeroom, she was pleasantly greeted by a pile of freshly harvested turnips. All the turnips Drukpa Kunley had eaten were in her storeroom.

'What a divine man,' she found herself saying aloud.

By this time, the divine man had reached the village of Chuyur.

The following day, Drukpa Kunley decided to erect a small stupa in the village single-handedly. He intended to finish it before nightfall. However, when the sun reacheed halfway between the zenith and the western horizon, he was only halfway through the task. So, he decided to arrest the sun's descent until the stupa was complete.

Nearby, a woman had spread her grains on a large flat rock to dry in the sun. She sat near the rock shooing away chickens and wild birds that came to peck at the grains.

'Today is an unusually long day,' she said to herself. Overhearing her, Drukpa Kunley interjected, 'Ama[32], the day is unusually long today, but nightfall is going to come suddenly.'

The woman glanced at Drukpa Kunley with indifference and then looked up into the sky. The sun was halfway between the

---

32 Mother or lady

zenith and the western horizon. She thought that the nondescript Tibetan stupa builder was teasing her.

The woman was dressed in a plain, white kira, an ankle-length dress wrapped around her body and secured at the waist with a large hand-woven belt called a kera. Round silver brooches fastened the upper ends of the kira to her shoulders. Beneath the kira, she wore a blouse known as a wonju. Perched on her head was a round bamboo hat, held in place by a thin string. Tucked into her kera at the back was a sickle with a long handle. She was barefoot, her toes splayed like claws, and she held a wooden walking staff.

'Ama, it's time to gather your grains,' Drukpa Kunley told her after an hour or so. His stupa had almost risen to its full height. 'Nightfall is going to come suddenly today,' he added.

The woman looked at Drukpa Kunley with annoyance and then looked up into the sky. The sun was still halfway between the zenith and the western horizon. She said, 'I can see the sun is still up there. How is your nightfall going to come suddenly?'

'Ama, I'm holding the sun in that position with an iron chain,' said Drukpa Kunley, gesturing as if pulling at a chain. The woman did not see any iron chain.

'Better build your stupa,' she said dismissively. 'I'll take care of my grains.'

After another hour or so, Drukpa Kunley's stupa was complete. He put a conical stone on it and said, 'Let this represent the sun and the moon.' Then he dusted his clothes and turned to the woman once again. 'Ama, it's time to gather your grains,' he said with a hint of a smile, 'because nightfall is going to come suddenly now.'

The woman turned away from Drukpa Kunley, irritated. The sun was still halfway between the zenith and the western horizon.

'All right,' Drukpa Kunley said with finality. 'I'm releasing the sun if you don't listen to me. My work is done, and I'm leaving.'

As Drukpa Kunley disappeared from the scene, the sun shot down the western sky and plunged behind the horizon.

Before the woman could gather a few handfuls of grains, it was pitch-dark.

CHAPTER 5
Shooting a Devotee Dead

It was a bright day in the hamlet of Chuyur in Paro, but the mood of its residents was sombre. The hamlet was recovering from a shocking incident it had witnessed six days ago. A Tibetan wanderer had shot Angay, a hundred-year-old woman from the village, with his arrow and locked up her body in a room. 'Do not open this room,' he had said. 'I'll be back in seven days to open it.'

A dozen villagers were sitting together listlessly in Angay's house—now weeping silently, now mumbling incoherent prayers. They talked little, but a sense of impatience pervaded the house.

'The body must be rotting, and that wanderer is nowhere to be seen,' one of them said, pulling on her rosary. Angay's son was highly suspicious of the wanderer, whom his late mother and some village elders believed to be an accomplished yogi. He would have broken the door of the room open if it hadn't been for his neighbours who stopped him.

However, as the afternoon wore on, Angay's son could no longer hold himself back; neither could anyone else. He picked up an iron hammer and broke the lock down with a swift blow.

Everyone stood behind him as he swung the door open. To everyone's astonishment, there was nothing under Angay's blanket except her right big toe. Everyone stood transfixed. Dumbfounded. Angay's son pulled the door close and slumped onto the floor.

Now, there was neither tear nor prayer; only pregnant silence.

The same group gathered in Angay's house the following morning. They were still trying to make sense of what had happened to Angay and her body.

As they sat and talked in hushed tones, in came the killer of the old woman, swift like a gust of wind. 'You've opened the door, haven't you?' he said, standing outside the room. 'This toe would have disappeared and joined Angay in the Blissful Pure Land if you had waited for me.'

Angay had attained what is known as the rainbow body. Certain accomplished Vajrayana practitioners are said to possess the ability to transmute their physical body into pure light, either before or after death. This extraordinary phenomenon involves either the transfer of the corporeal body to pure realms or a gradual shrinking of the body after death until it dissolves entirely. It symbolizes spiritual realization. Angay's unwavering devotion to Drukpa Kunley had helped her attain this realization.

Angay's friends, who had gathered at her house to offer chang to the wanderer a week ago, wept at the discovery.

As they stood in stunned silence, lost for words, the wanderer disappeared. They were left behind, overwhelmed by the moment. One of them dropped her rosary and prayer wheel and joined her palms on her forehead. Another shed a tear. Another, watery-eyed, prostrated after the man.

That was when they realized that, on that fateful day, the day they had wined and dined with the wanderer, Angay had seen in him what they had all missed.

※

Earlier that day, Angay was walking around the small stupa in the village, holding a prayer wheel in her right hand and a rosary in her left. With a hunched back, she leant heavily on a wooden staff. Her snow-white hair blended into the glistening white stupa's backdrop. She walked slowly and chanted, 'Om mani padmay hum. Homage to my lama.'

A Tibetan wanderer came prancing down the path. He froze mid-step the moment he saw Angay, his left hand on the hip and the right hand holding his bow like a walking staff. Angay darted a quick glance at him and continued to walk around the stupa chanting, 'Om mani pemay hum. Homage to my lama'. The man stood still until Angay came around and lightly brushed against him.

'Which lama are you praying to?' he asked Angay.

'Lama Drukpa Kunley,' answered Angay.

'Do you know him, and have you met him?'

Still walking, Angay turned and replied, 'I do not know him, and I've never met him. I've heard that he is a great naljorpa[33], so I'm praying to him.'

'What would you do if Drukpa Kunley were to appear before you right now?' asked the wanderer.

'I don't think I'll have the good fortune to meet the lama,' answered Angay. 'If, by chance, he were to come here right now, I would offer him all the food and chang I have since I'm too old to offer my body.'

'I am Drukpa Kunley,' the wanderer revealed.

Angay's initial reaction was one of disbelief as it was completely unexpected. For years, she had fervently prayed for the lama she had only heard about, but never did she imagine that her prayer would be answered in such a profound way. As she stood before him, a flood of emotions overwhelmed her. Tears welled up in her eyes, and her hands trembled with joy and incredulity. Her prayers had brought her face-to-face with the object of her devotion.

Unable to contain her overwhelming emotions, Angay sank to her knees and clutching Drukpa Kunley's feet, wept tears of devotion, begging him to provide her refuge at all time. She then

---

33 Yogi

invited him to her home and lavished food and chang upon him. She invited her friends from the village to meet Drukpa Kunley.

After eating and drinking to his heart's content, Drukpa Kunley asked Angay, 'Tell me now, old lady, how big is your devotion to me?' Angay said it was impossible to gauge her devotion to him, but she was even willing to die at his hands. Drukpa Kunley said that she was exaggerating, but she insisted that she meant it.

Then, he asked her to expose her side. He knew clairvoyantly that Angay was going to die that night anyway. As Angay raised her right hand and bared her side, Drukpa Kunley took his bow and arrow and shot her. As the arrow came out from the left side, Angay collapsed.

Angay's family and other people began yelling and howling that the wanderer was a wicked murderer. With last few breaths left, Angay begged that her lama, whom she held in pure devotion, be spared any accusation and hatred.

CHAPTER 6

The Undertaker Who Walks a Corpse to the Cremation Ground

The village of Jagarthang[34], covered in lush rice fields, lay along the banks of the Pachu River in Bhutan's western district of Paro. An ancient footpath ran right through the village across a mani dangrim, a long rectangular structure adorned with intricately carved stone slabs bearing the sacred mani mantra. Above the village, the landscape gradually transformed as gentle wooded slopes rose to meet the imposing foothills of majestic mountains.

A crowd had gathered in the middle of the rice fields. A blazing fire was burning under a huge pot balanced on three melon-sized rocks planted in a triangular formation. A few barefoot men with muscular calves stood near the pot. Each sipped from a cup.

Nearby, a group sat around a pot from which a young girl served with a wooden ladle. Everyone was talking loudly except for a middle-aged man who sat beside what looked like a heap of white cloth, gently fanning it with a sprig.

As Drukpa Kunley walked past the mani dangrim, one of the standing men transferred his cup to the left hand and waved his right hand, hollering, 'Hey man! Why don't you join us for some chang?'

Drukpa Kunley stopped abruptly, turned around and ambled towards the crowd, saying, 'Some chang during the summer season sounds refreshing.' He joined the noisy crowd and filled a wooden cup saying, 'Good chang is good for the body and a pleasant conversation is good for the mind.'[35]

Before Drukpa Kunley could ask the men why the crowd had gathered, a man minding the fire walked up to him and asked

---

34 Jagarthang has been erroneously translated into English as Indian plains because, literally, Jagarthang (རྒྱ་གར་ཐང་) means the plains of India.

35 ཆང་ཞིམ་པ་ལུས་ལ་ཕན། གཏམ་སྙན་པ་སེམས་ལ་ཕན།

if he would mind carrying Angay Akyi's body to the cremation ground. He pointed at the white heap. 'You look like a good, holy man.'

'Hey, come on! Don't you know that I'm not a beggar looking for an undertaker's job?' Drukpa Kunley said. 'Don't you know the saying, "Don't carry a corpse however much you crave food, don't masturbate however delighted you are?"'

The crowd fell silent.

The Pachu river tumbled towards Hungrel Dzong[36] some three hundred metres across the fields. A cow mooed by the bank. A red hen jumped out of its coop and cackled loudly. A cock preening in the shade answered the cackle and strutted towards the hen. Everybody glanced at the noisy birds and then identified a self-confident man in the crowd, signalling him to speak to Drukpa Kunley. The man stepped forward, hands by his sides and back slightly bent, to make the request. 'You are right, lama,' he said. 'It's the old woman's good fortune that has brought you here. Kindly bless her.'

'Please do,' the crowd pleaded with Drukpa Kunley.

'All right, then,' Drukpa Kunley agreed, 'I'll take her to the cremation ground. Where is it?'

The villagers pointed to the foot of a hill, a few kilometres above the village.

Gently whipping the corpse with a stick, Drukpa Kunley chanted:

---

36 The five-storey *dzong* was later offered to Zhabdrung Ngawang Namgyal who demolished it and built a new *dzong* in its place in 1646. The new *dzong*, named Rinpung Dzong, stands today as the Paro district administrative and monastic centre.

Arise, old soul, arise from slumber,
Arise from the mire of cyclic existence.
For no purpose, you've come into this world,
And with no purpose, you've taken your leave.
You know not where your free mind wanders,
Dropping your body before your children.
But willing undertakers, you have none.
Stripped of garments that veiled your nudity,
Your prized body now oozing nauseating fluids.
Lie not, old soul, arise and walk,
Walk along the path to liberation.

As he chanted these lines, the corpse gently rose and began walking towards the cremation ground. Drukpa Kunley followed it.

An old woman wiped her teary eyes and watery nose with her cuffs. Many joined their palms and raised them to the chest. Some simply held on to their empty cups. They followed the corpse, benumbed by the enormity of the moment with puzzled expressions on their faces.

Upon reaching the cremation ground, the corpse joined its palms in supplication and thanked Drukpa Kunley for liberating her. Then she lay on the pyre.

'Now cremate her,' Drukpa Kunley said.

As Drukpa Kunley prepared to leave, the grateful villagers hastily brought a pig's head and offered it to him. 'You will surely love it, for it makes a great dish,' they said. 'Do you have a pot to cook it?' They dropped the pig's head before him with a thud.

Drukpa Kunley pointed his right index finger at the pig's head and chanted:

> You swine of the ground floor sty,
> From head to tail, a hairy beast you are.
> On your nose sits a donkey's penis,
> You, too, must go from here,
> Follow the old woman now.

As he hit the pig's head with a finger, a ray of light departed from it and shot into the western sky visible to everyone.

The astonished villagers, deeply moved, showered Drukpa Kunley with offerings. However, he accepted none of them and promptly departed from the scene.

As he followed the old footpath towards Hungrel Dzong, he arrived at the hamlet of Gangtakha near the ancient temple of Kyerchu. Kyerchu Lhakhang is believed to have been built in mid-seventh century by Songtsen Gampo (c. 605–650), the thirty-second king of the Yarlung dynasty of Tibet. Kyerchu Lhakhang and Jampa Lhakhang in Bumthang, known to be the earliest temples in Bhutan, are among the one hundred and eight temples believed to have been built by King Songtsen Gampo to tame a demoness lying supine across the Himalayan region.

In Gangtakha, Lama Tshewang[37] had just finished constructing a magnificent new house. As Drukpa Kunley passed by the hamlet, Lama Tshewang requested him to sprinkle grains around his new house and bless it with a special prayer.

---

37 Lama Tshewang may have been a son of Phajo Drukgom Zhigpo's great-great grandson, Drung Drung Gyalzom, who settled and started his lineage in Gangtakha hamlet in Paro. In one of his biographies, Drukpa Kunley describes his contemporary Drung Drung Gyalzom as an irreligious man with wrong views.

The double-storey house, built with timber, stone and mud, was a fine specimen of traditional Bhutanese architecture. The walls of the ground floor were built with rammed mud. The first floor was one solid wooden frame with large, intricately designed windows. Delicately carved timber lintels and cornices separated the ground floor, first floor and the roof. The roof, clad with wooden shingles anchored by melon-sized rocks, spread like protective wings. Every inch of the wooden framework was painted with dazzling colours.

Drukpa Kunley gladly agreed to the request and said any new house must be blessed with the right prayer. He did not carry customary religious instruments for an elaborate ceremony, but simply sprinkled a handful of rice around the house. As he did so, he chanted a unique prayer:

> For the door is solid like the hills,
> May the house be as firm as the hills.
> For bow-shaped bands rest on columns,
> May the house stand on strong support.
> For the beams and rafters are straight,
> May the house be honest and upright.
> For the roof spreads like protective wings,
> May the house be secure and protected.

Concluding the prayer, he added, 'May this house be blessed with plenty of people and plenty of corpses.'

In Bhutanese culture, a large family, which naturally means many deaths, is traditionally seen as a sign of prosperity. However, Lama Tshewang interpreted the blessing literally, fearing it meant a large number of deaths in his family. 'How unsettling!' he exclaimed. 'This is not an auspicious prayer. Corpses should not even be mentioned for it will bring bad luck.'

Drukpa Kunley simply smiled and said, 'Well, if you don't like that blessing, I can offer you another. May the house be blessed with few people and few corpses.'

Relieved by this alternative, Lama Tshewang readily accepted it. He thanked Drukpa Kunley for the new blessing, 'You have put it very well.'

'Not really,' Drukpa Kunley rejoined.

As time passed, Lama Tshewang's family began to dwindle. With each passing year, there were fewer and fewer family members until the lineage eventually died out completely.

CHAPTER 7

A Hammer that Inflicts a Rotting Wound

All was calm. The late afternoon breeze swept across the verdant hillside as the dappled sun rays slowly climbed their way up the hill. The man lay still, eyes gently closed as if half asleep.

His penis was erect and upright. He was lying supine on a grassy patch amid whispering chir pine trees, his stomach sunken deep into his ribcage. He had a bow, a quiver and a sword for a pillow. A few strands of his long, tousled hair swayed in the breeze. Beside him sat a bag of roasted barley flour. His legs were apart and knees slightly bent so that his anus, dusted with barley flour, was exposed. He was stark naked.

Soon, someone stomped towards the sleeping man and squinted at him curiously. 'Oh!' he cried in fright. 'I've never seen such a thing before, but it must be something good to feast on.'

At long last, he called out to his friends in a thundering voice that echoed across the hillside. In an instant, innumerable demons of the hillside heeded their master's call and swarmed in from all directions like flies on rotten meat.

'He is dead,' one bellowed.

'No, he is alive,' another corrected him.

'Wait,' the spirit from the upper reaches of Dago Gonpa, the place where the strange man was sleeping, interrupted. 'I'm not sure if we should eat him up. He appears dead, but his body is warm. He appears alive, but he isn't breathing. He seems to have died from hunger, but there is flour nearby. He may not have died of gluttony because his stomach has sagged.'

The other spirits nodded in agreement silently. The sleeping man remained still and quiet. His weather-beaten face appeared peaceful. The spirits gazed at him and then turned to their friend, who was trying to make sense of the strange man.

'He may not have died of fear,' the spirit from the upper reaches of the hill continued, 'because he is equipped with a bow and arrows. He may not have died long ago because his penis is erect and hard. But it has certainly been a while since he died because maggots have started feeding on his putrid anus. Let's leave him alone, for he doesn't bode well for us.'

The spirits agreed to leave the sleeping man alone but decided to make a meal of the old woman in Wang Gonsakha village after nightfall. The village was only half an hour's walk from Dago Gonpa.

The sleeping man had been listening and discovered what the demons were up to that night.

'You are a good religious person,' the trembling, old woman of Gonsakha said as she opened the door for the stranger seeking shelter for the night. 'I don't want you, my guest, to be eaten by the hungry demons along with me. Go away from this village tonight. Return later, after I'm gone, to claim my wealth and use it for your religious pursuit.'

It was dusk and already dark inside, but the old woman had not lit the pine wood shavings on the flat stone placed on a block of wood sitting near the hearth. She had closed all the windows to shut out the thickening darkness that would bring demons to her.

Outside, there was no sign of humans or animals. A typical farming village in Bhutan comes alive at dusk when the cows come home mooing and the farmers return from the fields cheerfully humming old tunes. But not a soul stirred in Wang Gonsakha village today.

'Do not worry about me, my hostess,' the guest said, sliding in sideways to avoid his bow and arrows brushing against the woman standing in the doorway. The doddering woman found the roughly clad guest foolhardy. 'He's unnecessarily laying his life on the line,' she thought, looking at the man who slumped heavily on the floor near the hearth. He sat there, looking calm and relaxed.

'Instead, give me chang if you have some,' the guest requested in a reassuring tone. 'You can sit in a corner. I will deal with whatever comes our way.'

The old woman brought a wooden container of chang and unsteadily splashed some into a wooden cup. 'Its flavour must have been soaked up by the demons who have emptied the village. Not even an animal is spared. I await my turn tonight.'

As the guest quietly sipped chang with relish, heavy thudding sounds, accompanied by grunts and snorts, shattered the silence of the night. The old woman shrieked and recoiled into a corner, petrified. The guest reassuringly gesticulated to the woman to stay put in the corner.

He poured himself another cup of chang. The commotion outside became louder and hysterical by the second. In a few moments, there was a veritable stampede at the doorstep. A noisy demon was stomping its feet and banging and pushing the door.

The rickety wooden door creaked, rattled, and clonked but refused to give way. A snarling, drooling red mouth stretched wide open with interlocking fangs could be seen from a fist-sized hole in the door.

Crouched in the corner, the old woman was too horrified to look at the door. The guest, now pressing himself against the door, looked agitated. His calm face twitched and turned grave, and his eyes were filled with intense power. In a flash, he thrust his red penis into the demon's mouth and knocked out eight teeth, four each from the lower and upper gums.

The demon let out a yelp and fled the scene, shrieking and squealing, 'Something has hit my mouth!'

It was midnight.

'At the old woman's house in Gonsakha was a fellow who was neither a layman nor a monk. His groin hid a flaming iron hammer, which hit me,' the demon explained to Ani[38] Samten Palmo, who was meditating in the cave of Singye Gyeltshen, a rocky hillside below Dagala, about a day's walk from Wang Gonsakha village. The Cave of Singye Gyeltshen is a sacred hermitage blessed and sanctified by Drukpa hierarch Phajo Drukgom Zhigpo (1184?–1251?), who had meditated there for six months almost three centuries ago.

The demon had bounded down the rocky mountainside below Gonsakha, crossed the Wangchu river, and climbed up the opposite mountainside to meet the lone practitioner to seek her help.

He was writhing in agony before the nun, his mouth open, exposing the bloody, toothless gums. The flesh-eating terror of Gonsakha was now pale and shaking like a hounded animal.

Seated in the lotus position on a thin cushion of dry grass, Ani Samten was the reverse image of the demon. She was calm and showed no emotion. She slowly wore her rosary around her neck and inspected the wound. She spoke slowly and clearly, 'Hmm, your mouth has been hit by something strange. It can never be cured.'

She stretched and opened her legs wide and pulled her maroon wrap-around right up to the navel to bare her vagina. 'If you don't

---

38 Nun

believe me,' she added, 'look at this wound inflicted by the same flaming hammer. It can never be cured.'

The demon became curious and stopped groaning momentarily. He leaned forward and stared at the organ, sprang upright and squinted at it. Then he deftly dipped a finger into the ani's vagina and brought it to his nose. 'Yuck! Your wound is rotten,' he snorted, spitting out and flinging his hand. 'Is my wound going to rot like yours?'

Ani Samten drew her legs together and told the demon that there was a remedy against his wound rotting. 'Go back to the same house immediately and submit yourself to the man wielding the flaming hammer, who is Drukpa Kunley,' she instructed. 'Offer him your life and take an oath never to take life again.'

With his mouth wound healed, that demon lives to this day among the ruins of Wang Gonsakha village as a dharma protector under oath. His name is Langdud.

CHAPTER 8

The Burial of Dochula's Terror

THE BURIAL OF DOCHULA'S TERROR | 39

An eighteen-year-old lad was desperately trying to cross the Dochula Pass as fast as he could. He was flogging an old bull that was slowing him down. The bull clopped and puffed before him but hardly covered any ground.

The lad looked agitated. He was racing against the setting sun. As he hit the crest of the mountain with his bull, the sun disappeared behind the horizon.

Before him stretched miles of wilderness into which the narrow footpath that would take him home disappeared. His village of Wang Barma could not even be seen.

As he looked back, Talo and Nobgang villages were little white specks against a dark blue hill. He murmured a few words of prayer. In the distance gleamed some of the highest mountain ranges, at once inviting and formidable.

Right before him rose a mighty moss-laden tree. Nightfall was near, but his home was far. The bull didn't care. A sense of foreboding overwhelmed him.

As he exasperatedly flogged his bull, a strangely confident man appeared before him. He walked briskly. He carried a bow in his left hand and a quiver slung across his back.

'Where are you headed, young man?' asked the confident man.

'I'm on my way home with this sluggish old bull,' replied the lad. 'Could you please help me get home?'

'Why do you need help?'

'The dreaded demoness of Dochula will surely waylay me, and this bull is slowing me down,' replied the lad, trembling.

'Don't worry. You can rush home. I'll take care of your bull—'

'But it will be dark before I reach home.'

'Here is how you can reach home safely,' the man said. He asked the lad to lie on his lap and think about his home. As the lad put his head on the man's lap and visualized his home, he was instantly teleported to Wang Barma.

It was dark now. The ancient forest came alive with the sounds of nocturnal birds and insects. The man took his time to tether the bull to the tree and climb up into its branches.

Towards midnight, a hefty figure came stomping by and stopped near the bull. It was the demoness of Dochula. She stared at the bull with great curiosity. She looked around and nodded with assurance. She turned uphill and shouted, 'There's something to eat. Come forth.' Then she turned downhill and shouted her invitation into the night. The hills echoed. The old bull turned around to glance at the demoness but continued to chew on cud.

In an instant, the demonesses of Singlila and Hinglila came whizzing by. As the three demonesses prepared to make a meal of the old bull, a heavy branch thudded onto the ground between them, which startled them. They looked up and spotted the man who had hurled the branch.

'Climb down, dear. Let's hang out together,' the demonesses said in unison.

'I'm not in a mood to hang out with you. You all are disgusting,' the man told them in an insulting tone.

'What insolence,' the demoness of Dochula yelled, looking at her friends. 'Bring him down.'

The infuriated demonesses bit through the trunk of the tree with sheer ferocity. As the tree came crashing down, so did the man's penis, hard and flaming, on the demonesses. That was when they discovered that the man who had dared to speak back to them was Drukpa Kunley.

The demonesses of Singlila and Hinglila dissolved into the demoness of Toebisa and vanished from the scene. Drukpa Kunley caught the demoness of Dochula by her hair and dragged her downhill towards Wangdi all night. She screamed and wailed and begged for mercy. When she lost her voice, she whimpered miserably. But Drukpa Kunley was determined to punish her for her atrocities.

At dawn, when they reached Lobesa, the helpless demoness transformed into a red dog to escape. But Drukpa Kunley dragged the dog by the ear to a nearby hillock and buried it there. He built a black stupa at the burial spot and prophesied that a temple would rise from there. Later in 1499, illustrious Lama Ngawang Chogyal is believed to have built a temple on the spot, which came to be known as Khyimay[39] Lhakhang, a temple more associated with Drukpa Kunley than its builder.

Sometime later, Drukpa Kunley went to Wang to meet Barbi Chozom, one of his favourite Bhutanese maidens. After spending a few days with her, one morning, he set off to Tshelungna.

That afternoon in Tshelungna, Drukpa Kunley found himself in a dire predicament. With most people having gone to Wang for iron ore mining, most houses were securely locked, leaving him without a place to spend the night.

Tshelungna was a sacred site blessed over the centuries by numerous spiritual luminaries, including Padmasambhava, popularly known as Guru Rinpoche in Bhutan, Khandro Yeshe Tshogyal, and Phajo Drukgom Zhigpo. That was the place where Pachang Namkha Drolma, Drukpa Kunley's consort from Lobesa, meditated and gained liberation. It was a wilderness roamed by formidable creatures like big cats and bears. Drukpa Kunley needed to find a safe place for the night, yet none of the remaining residents invited him.

---

39 ཁྱི་མེད། (Literally 'no dog')

Towards early evening, a lone woman named Dondrub Zangmo, a devout practitioner, approached Drukpa Kunley and invited him to her house. He asked her if she had chang. She said she had seven measures. 'I will pay you generously for your chang,' he assured her.

Drukpa Kunley sat back, relishing chang and smiling broadly. 'Do you have any miner in Wang from your family?' he asked her.

'My twenty-three-year-old son Tshering Wangyal is among the miners,' she replied.

'In that case, put your mouth to that empty pot and call him,' he told her.

At that moment, Tshering Wangyal was toiling away in the pit. As his mother called his name into the pot, he heard his name being called. He immediately emerged from the pit to answer the call. As soon as he was on the surface, the walls of the pit collapsed, burying twenty-nine men alive.

Tshering Wangyal instantly rushed home to find his mother engaged in conversation with Drukpa Kunley. 'Did you call me when I was in the pit?' he asked his mother, still out of breath.

'Yes, I called your name into that pot,' she confirmed. 'Where are your friends?'

'They were all buried in the mine,' he said.

'Your son would have been among them,' Drukpa Kunley told Dondrub Zangmo. 'You were a good host and gave me chang. This is the payment for your chang.'

Dondrub Zangmo could not believe the invaluable prize her chang had earned. Bursting with joy, she could not sit still and talk without fidgeting. 'There is no way I can thank you enough for your kindness,' she said. 'If I had horses and bulls, I'm most willing to offer them all to you.'

CHAPTER 9

The Deliverance of Wola Gyap Tenzin

The village of Wolakha in Bhutan's western district of Punakha pulsated with a mixture of sounds. A disconsolate calf bleated from the middle of the terraced paddy fields on the outskirts of the village. Its mother grunted and mooed in response. A colourful rooster crowed spiritedly from a rafter of a hay barn as a few hens cackled around him. The low sound of a drum boomed from a house.

Faint sounds of people calling out to one another could be heard from the opposite hillock across the Toebi Rongchu stream. Some distance from the hillock flowed Puna Tsangchu, calm and blue. A thirty-minute walk down, a mule track led one to the confluence of Toebi Rongchu and Puna Tsangchu where a dreaded demoness, Longrong Dudmo, lived.

Drukpa Kunley had just subdued the water demoness Longrong Dudmo and put her on the dharma path. But when he walked down to her dwelling, Longrong Dudmo mocked Drukpa Kunley as a purposeless wanderer. She emerged from the middle of the river in a terrifying form and sang.

> Mount Kailash, fabled and famed,
> A fort wild, cold and unpeopled.
> What is wondrous about this peak,
> Mere earth and rock clad in snow?

> The white snow lion, fabled and famed,
> Flaunting white fur and a flowing mane.
> What is wondrous about a mere animal
> Roaring away in desolate, wild valleys?

THE DELIVERANCE OF WOLA GYAP TENZIN

> Jatang Kunley, fabled and famed,
> A purposeless wandering destitute.
> What is wondrous about a prattler
> Who indulges in worthless chatter?

Drukpa Kunley stood at the river bank, his right foot perched on a large rock. Before him, the demoness loomed large, floating on the rushing waters. To make himself heard above the river's roar, he had to raise his voice. He extended his right hand towards her and spoke.

> Mount Kailash is fabled and famed
> For it is home to five hundred arhats[40].

> The white snow lion is fabled and famed
> For it's the steed of mamos[41] and dakinis.

> Jatang Kunley is fabled and famed
> For I'm the object of worship for all.
> I'm a purposeless wandering destitute
> For I've cast away all worldly desires.

> I utter whatever comes to my mind
> For I destroy hypocrisy masked as truth.
> I indulge in crazy antinomic behaviour
> For I liberate beings in diverse ways.

---

40 དགྲ་བཅོམ་པ་: Literally 'foe destroyer', one who has completely overcome all emotions and thus liberated. Arhat is also used as an epithet of Lord Buddha.

41 A class of female deities.

> Milarepa and I, Kunley, turn situations,
> Good and bad, into mental ornaments.
> You, Longrong Dudmo Choechong Kyi,
> Beings like gods, nagas, goblins, demons
> Can be my consort, charming as they are.

Drukpa Kunley then urged Longrong Dudmo to follow his path to attain liberation within a lifetime. She was instantly won over by Drukpa Kunley's charisma and charm. She metamorphosed into a beautiful maiden, enticing him with her self-proclaimed unmatched sexual prowess. She said, for a yogi who loved sex, a lustful naga spirit could offer the ultimate experience.

After Longrong Dudmo vowed never to harm any living being, Drukpa Kunley accepted her as his spiritual consort through a sexual union. For a yogi who had completely realized and internalized the nonduality of things, a sexual union with a non-human was not out of place.

Drukpa Kunley had outgrown the conventional confines of dualistic thinking. For him, there was no difference between human and non-human consorts. As the literal meaning of the Choekey term for nonduality, 'nyimay'[42] or 'not two', showed, things did not exist in contrasting pairs, such as good and evil, purity and impurity, beautiful and ugly. There was no inherent dichotomy. Everything embodied a unity. He believed that humans and demons were not disparate entities but rather two facets of the same reality. They were inseparable, akin to the two sides of a coin. Without one, the other could not exist. A human

---

42 གཉིས་མེད།

was defined by the absence of demonhood, and vice versa. Their identities were intertwined.

Over time, Longrong Dudmo grew deeply attached to Drukpa Kunley. However, when Drukpa Kunley took Pachang Namkha Drolma as another consort, Longrong Dudmo was consumed by jealousy and turned against him. Yet, she was once again subdued and transformed into the dharma protector known as Dzombu Kyi.

One day, Drukpa Kunley came up the mule track leading to Longrong Dudmo's dwelling. He walked briskly with his dog following him. As he reached a barren stretch of land called Lokthang Chamo near Wolakha, an old man named Wola Gyap[43] Tenzin prostrated before him.

'Everybody who meets you is immensely fortunate,' he said. 'I'm a happy man, having brought up all my children and sent the youngest to a monastery. What I desire now is that dharma be my refuge when my time comes.'

Drukpa Kunley looked at Wola Gyap Tenzin with curiosity and compassion. Wola Gyap Tenzin was of medium build. His face was heavily wrinkled, his hair grey, and his red-rimmed eyes were watery. He wore his gho[44] high above the knees and dangled a dagger down his right thigh. He was barefoot. Fresh mud stuck between his toes made his feet look webbed.

Wola Gyap Tenzin lived a life of simplicity, honesty and good intentions. Although he did not say regular prayers, he had contemplated on the transitory nature of life and living

---

43 The old man of Wolakha. Previously, Gyap (རྒོད་པོ་) has been erroneously written as Gyalpo (རྒྱལ་པོ་) or king. Tenzin was not a king but an ordinary elderly man.

44 The traditional Bhutanese dress for men.

throughout his adult life. His only aspiration was to nurture his children with affection and compassion, while spreading good intentions within his small circle. With age, he meditated on his inevitable mortality and how best to prepare his mind for that eventuality. Drukpa Kunley recognized him as a noble man the moment he looked at him.

'All right,' Drukpa Kunley said. 'Chant this refuge prayer whenever you think of me. You don't need to be embarrassed about it.'

> Homage to the old man's indefatigable penis, fallen like an aged tree yet strong in will not to yield;
> Homage to the old woman's unrelenting vagina, sunken like a deep gorge yet strong in will not to yield;
> Homage to the young man's audacious penis, unafraid and undaunted by death when driven by arrogance;
> Homage to the young woman's unflinching vagina, undeterred and unashamed when driven by a flood of desire.

'Thank you very much indeed,' the old man said, beaming with joy. 'Now, please teach me an aspiration prayer.'

'All right,' Drukpa Kunley said, and chanted this prayer.

> The foliage of the mighty tree of the east appears to grow and spread;
> Whether the foliage actually grows and spreads, only the tree can tell you.
> To Kunley's penis with a large head, a little vagina appears tight and firm;
> Whether the vagina is actually tight and firm, only the large-headed penis can tell you.

To you, the devoted old man, liberation appears within reach;
Whether liberation is actually within reach, only your devotion
can tell you.

The old man prostrated three times before Drukpa Kunley, chanting the prayer in a shaky voice. He felt a quiver of devotion run through him as he ambled home.

'Did you meet the lama and receive teaching from him, Apa[45]?' asked his daughter.

'Of course, I did,' the old man said as he sat cross-legged by the living room window. 'He taught me a refuge prayer which I've learnt by heart.'

'This prayer must be short and easy because you are not intelligent enough to memorize a lengthy prayer so quickly,' teased his daughter. 'Can you chant it for us?'

Wola Gyap tucked the ends of his gho under his thighs, sat upright, joined his palms into a lotus shape, closed his eyes, and chanted the refuge prayer solemnly: Homage to the old man's indefatigable penis, fallen like an aged tree yet strong in will not to yield …

The daughter reddened and rushed out. His wife looked at him angrily, her face twitching in disapproval tinged with amusement. 'You've gone crazy, old man,' she admonished him. 'A lama's teaching cannot be so vulgar. You've either misunderstood him or forgotten his teaching. Even if these are the very words of the lama, you should never repeat them before our children.'

The old man sat with an air of confidence. He said, 'These are the very words of my lama, who has instructed me to chant this prayer whenever I think of him. I don't care what you think of it.'

---

45 Father

Later that day, when the family gathered for dinner, Wola Gyap joined his palms, closed his eyes and began: Homage to the old man's indefatigable penis, fallen like an aged tree yet strong in will not to yield …

Everybody picked up their food and walked out, saying, 'Apa has certainly lost his mind.'

His wife returned to caution him against repeating his prayer. But the old man insisted that he must continue chanting the prayer even at the cost of his life. 'So be it then,' his wife said with finality. 'If you persist with this madness, you must live away from us.'

The following day, Wola Gyap was taken to the family's hay barn on a hillock above the village. But the family never missed him. They could hear him faintly chanting his refuge prayer day and night.

Drukpa Kunley created a small spring near the hay barn for Wola Gyap. The spring babbled and cascaded down the hillside of Wolakha village, disappearing below thick bushes at some places, sparkling into view at others, and peeping through leaves and branches at some spots. The spring water was imbued with special qualities that satiated Wola Gyap's hunger and thirst. As he drank the cool and refreshing spring water, he felt a divine sense of fulfilment, nourishment and awareness.

About a month later, at the dawn of the full moon day, Wola Gyap suddenly fell silent, and the delightful sounds of lute and flute drifted from the hay barn. The wife was worried that the old man might have swooned from making excessive noise continuously. So, she asked her daughter to take him some chang.

Inside the barn, Wola Gyap was nowhere to be found. There was only a heap of quilt. Under the quilt was a ball of rainbow light with a white letter 'ah' (ཨ) glowing in the centre. The astounded daughter screamed and wailed that her father was dead.

As the village gathered around the barn, the ball of light rose into the eastern sky accompanied by the voice of Wola Gyap Tenzin that said, 'Drukpa Kunley has delivered me to Potala, the paradise of Avalokiteshvara. You, the prudish lot, may stay back. Offer my Lokthang Chamo to Lama Drukpa Kunley.'

CHAPTER 10

The Birth of the Goat-headed Bull

Shar Luetshogang in the Wangdi district of western Bhutan was abuzz that day. More than seven thousand people from across Bhutan were milling about in the morning sun. There were lamas, nuns, the elderly, and fresh-faced maidens. Everybody looked greatly curious and expectant.

In front of the crowd spread the enchanting Luetsho Lake, green and sparkling. The lake is believed to have settled over a farmer's barley field. The tale goes that, one night, a beautiful girl volunteered to watch over the tired farmer's barley field. When the farmer returned to his field the following morning, it had turned into a lake.

Beyond the hills lay the inviting villages of Shar. Kunzangling, Kazhi, Chungseygang and Phangyul dotted the hillsides like little fairylands. Like thousands from other villages across Bhutan, people from these villages had walked to Luetshogang, present-day Samtengang, to see Drukpa Kunley.

Drukpa Kunley sat in the crowd, chatting casually. He wore scanty clothing but a lavish smile. His bow and arrows lay beside him, and his dog, before him. His bow and arrows symbolize the destruction of ten classes of enemies, and the hunting dog symbolizes hunting down and destroying dualistic tendencies.

Little children chased one another past him, stirring up clouds of dust, but he was not bothered. He smiled and sipped his chang.

'All of you look radiant today,' he said to the fair maidens surrounding him. Around him were Anan Dhara, Chungsey Ache Gyalzom, Wachen Bumo Goeked Palzom, Gontoe Ache Adzom, Pachang Namkha Drolma, Wangza Choezom, Sharmo Kunzangmo, and many other girls who were connected to him.

'Lama la[46],' some devotees requested, 'we've heard wonderful stories about your miraculous powers, but we've never seen you perform a miracle.'

'Kindly let us witness your miracle, lama la,' some more devotees requested him.

Outwardly, Drukpa Kunley seemed uninhibited, even interested, in the public display of miracles and clairvoyance. But inwardly, he often cringed in hesitation. Public display of supernatural abilities is discouraged for Vajrayana practitioners because onlookers might be too ordinary to grasp or fathom phenomena beyond the confines of their mundane world. When miracles are too big for their little minds[47], they could be misunderstood or, worse still, misconstrued as magical tricks wrought by some mundane, invisible spirits behind the person.

This possibility was particularly stark for Drukpa Kunley, who only seemed to drink, sing and spend time with girls without any spiritual practice. Yet, the public display of supernatural powers could act as a powerful agent of transformation for some people endowed with enough merit and broadmindedness, or 'spacious interior of the mind'[48], to absorb them.

'All right,' said Drukpa Kunley, for the sake of the latter group of people. He was neither excited nor daunted by the request.

---

46 In Bhutan, suffix *la* added at the end of a phrase or sentence denotes respect. Although there is no practice of adding *la* after a person's name as a mark of respect like Tibetans do, the Bhutanese add *la* after a title such as lama as a symbol of their veneration.

47 བློ་སྨ་ཆུང་བ།

48 བློ་ཁོག་ཡངས་པ།

In the meantime, lunch was served. It was a gargantuan one for Drukpa Kunley—one solid head of a goat and one whole carcass of a bull.

Everybody looked on as Drukpa Kunley sat before a mountain of meat several times the size of his own body. He rubbed his palms with relish. Conjuring up an appetite matching the amount of food, he devoured the meat with relish.

'A hearty meal it was,' said Drukpa Kunley, smiling and wiping his mouth. 'Thank you.'

Without a morsel of meat sticking to the bones, before him lay the skull of a goat and the skeleton of a bull.

The devotees looked at the smiling Drukpa Kunley and then at the heap of bare bones, wide-eyed. It was truly miraculous, they said. They whispered to one another, trying to understand what the superhuman feat they had just witnessed meant. They said that either Drukpa Kunley or the mountain of meat must be unreal and delusional.

Just then, Drukpa Kunley picked up the goat's skull and stuck it to the bull's skeleton, admiring the odd combination like a self-absorbed sculptor.

Then he snapped his fingers and said, 'There's no flesh on your body. Go eat grass.' At this, the bull's skeleton stood up and, carrying the goat's skull, walked up the hill and disappeared into the forest.

The devotees were stunned. Some prostrated before Drukpa Kunley. Some simply looked at him with great admiration and devotion. But wonderment overpowered their sense of devotion.

The stocky bovine increased in number and spread across north-western Bhutan. They are often described as unique animals with the head of a goat and the body of a bull.

Years later, the descendants of these devotees would call the offspring of this strange goat-headed animal born of Drukpa Kunley's meal drong gyimtsi or takin, the national animal of Bhutan.

༄

The devotees then implored Drukpa Kunley for a teaching that combined the sacred with the profane, the religious with the secular—a discourse both profound and easy to remember.

'Are you prepared to receive a teaching full of penises and vaginas?' Drukpa Kunley asked.

'Nothing that flows from your lips is meaningless,' replied the devotees. 'Everything you utter transforms into precious wisdom.'

'If you have the good humour and appetite for my madness, I shall impart a few words,' Drukpa Kunley said, before breaking into a stream of verses with natural ease and spontaneity. He employed a distinctive style, weaving religious and secular ideas with colourful and provocative language. Each ribald line alluded to a sacred truth. The devotees listened intently, hanging on to every word.

> In Sanskrit, my penis goes sharara[49]
> In Tibetan, girls' vaginas go shururu[50].
> Here's the discourse on worldly delights:
>
> Young girls delight in a deluge of desire,
> Young men delight in satiating that desire,
> The old delight in reliving fond memories;

---

49 Continuously and unobstructed.
50 Smoothly and unhindered.

I shall teach through these three delights.

For bed is the factory for sex,
Let it be comfortable and wide.
For the knee is the messenger of sex,
Let it go over her well in advance.
For hands are the harness of sex,
Let them go around her tightly.
For hips are the hub of ecstasy,
Let them heave again and again.
This is the discourse on permissibles.

It's wrong to make love to a wedded woman,
It's wrong to make love to a girl not yet ten,
It's wrong to make love to a celibate woman,
A woman in period, pregnant, or grieving;
This is the discourse on three impermissibles.

Whosoever is destitute has a big appetite,
Whosoever is foolish has a big dick,
Whosoever is a woman has a big lust;
This is the discourse on three big things.

'Ah, this reference to women's lust is so true,' chuckled a middle-aged man, his grin revealing teeth stained with the crimson hue of betel juice.

'And what about the reference to foolish men's size?' retorted a woman sitting near him, her playful banter directed at all men around her. A ripple of laughter swept through the crowd as they gestured to each other to resume listening to Drukpa Kunley, who continued:

Whosoever is old has little imagination,
Whosoever is orphaned has little merit,
Whosoever is rich has little generosity;
This is the discourse on three little things.

All lamas find joy in offerings,
All lords find joy in flattery,
All girls find joy in lovers;
This is the discourse on three joys.

Sinners love to hate the devout,
The rich love to hate the generous,
Wives love to hate the unfaithful;
This is the discourse on three hatreds.

Worship lamas who are sublime,
Worship deities who grant blessings,
Worship guardians who do virtuous deeds;
This is the discourse on three worships.

There is self-liberation in gentle manners,
There is compassion in the absence of self-love,
There is Tantra in understanding primordial unity;
This is the discourse on three things present.

The greedy lack contentment,
The worldly-wise lack the dharma,
The village roamers lack vows;
This is the discourse on three lackings.

Those without facts don't file a lawsuit,
Those without samaya don't worship lamas,

THE BIRTH OF THE GOAT-HEADED BULL

Those without courage don't become generals;
This is the discourse on three don'ts.

Whosoever is rich has a tight fist,
Whosoever is old has a tight mind,
Whosoever is a nun has a tight vagina;
This is the discourse on three tight things.

Smooth talkers find themselves inside crowds,
Offerings find themselves inside monks' mouths,
Large penises find themselves inside girls' vaginas;
This is the discourse on three things found inside others.

The mind of bodhisattvas is softer than wool,
Just like the talk of self-serving people.
The thighs of girls are softer than silk;
This is the discourse on three soft things.

Thin is the skirt of immoral monks,
So is sustenance for loveless women,
Thin are crops not nourished by manure;
This is the discourse on three thin things.

Drukpa Kunley is never satiated by girls,
Girls are never satiated by penises,
Monks are never satiated by offerings;
This is the discourse on three unsatiated things.

Drukpa Kunley paused, casting a dazzling smile upon the assembled devotees. A soft chuckle rippled through the crowd. The monks exchanged whispers among themselves, acknowledging,

'His jibe is targeted at us.' They smiled sheepishly, too, embarrassed to join the chuckles. Drukpa Kunley continued.

> However brilliant, a disciple needs a lama,
> However luminous, a lamp needs good oil,
> However clear, the mind needs awareness.
>
> Laughable is a lama with no devotees
> As is a disciple with no diligence.
> Laughable is an unheeded order
> As is a woman who is unwooed.
>
> Laughable is a lord with no servants
> As is a rich man with no generosity.
> Laughable is a farmer with no crops
> As is a nomad with no livestock.
>
> Laughable is a monk with no vows
> As is a hermit with no learning.
> Laughable is a nun craving sex
> As is a man with no erection.
>
> Laughable is wealth earned through sex
> As is a lustful girl too prudish for pleasure.

After a prolonged, deliberate pause, as if priming the gathering for something more risqué, he continued:

> The clitoris may boast a beautiful triangular shape
> But it is unsuitable as an offering to local deities.

Vaginal fluid may not vaporize under the sun's heat
But it cannot be used to brew tea to quench thirst.

The scrotums may be full and loaded and heavy
But they cannot serve as provisions for hermits.

The penis may have a strong shaft and a large head
But it cannot be used to hammer stakes into the ground.

One may be endowed with a beautiful human form
But it cannot be offered as a bride for the Lord of Death.

One may be well-disposed towards sublime dharma
But practise one cannot from the comfort of home.

The sacred teachings of Vajrayana may be profound
But sans practice, liberation remains far and elusive.

I, Kunley, may show you the path to liberation
But the stairways you must ascend on your own.

Drukpa Kunley's words inspired profound devotion to dharma among the devotees, eliciting both tears and laughter. An elderly man from the crowd stepped forward, remarking, 'Your teachings are as accessible, lucid, deep, and captivating as Luetsho lake itself. Only the teachings of a buddha can be so multifaceted.'

CHAPTER 11
The Mad Yogi Who Urinated Gold

THE MAD YOGI WHO URINATED GOLD

Two men, a Bhutanese and a Tibetan, were intently poring over an exquisite thangka[51] depicting Kagyu Serthreng, the unbroken lineage of the Kagyu school of Buddhism. The Bhutanese man, eighty-year-old Sumdar, looked markedly different from the Tibetan man. Sumdar was demure and self-effacing. The Tibetan was bald-faced and cocky. They squatted beside the footpath leading to Ralung in Tibet.

They bumped into each other in the middle of a vast, desolate hillside. The Tibetan was heading south, while the Bhutanese was heading north.

The air was thin and biting. Sparse vegetation clung tenaciously to life, with hardy grasses, shrubs and occasional patches of stunted trees dotting the landscape.

The Tibetan man, a veritable beggar with a spiritual streak, showed no particular interest in the thangka. Yet, he asked Sumdar to unfurl it on the ground.

'Hmm, not a bad thing at all,' the Tibetan observed. Sumdar joined his palms and placed them on his chest, eyes downcast, in deep reverence to the thangka.

The thangka was crowded with scores of colourful images arranged in the shape of a tree. It depicted the central figure of Vajradhara, the primordial Buddha, in dark blue colour surrounded by the saints of the Kagyu lineage, including Bengali saints Tilopa and Naropa, and Tibetan saints Marpa and Milarepa. The images were set against an expansive background, complete with the earth and water, the sky and clouds, gods and deities and humans

---

51 A *thangka* is a traditional Buddhist painting done on cotton, silk, or canvas that depicts deities, mandalas, scenes from the life of the Buddha, or other aspects of Buddhist cosmology. *Thangkas* serve as both visual aids for meditation and objects of veneration and are usually framed in rich brocade silk.

and animals. For Sumdar, the thangka represented the sum of all of these elements.

But for all its flawless symmetry and elegance, the thangka did not have a gold overlay.

'So, you are taking this to Lama Ngawang Chogyal?' asked the Tibetan man.

'Yes. I wish to have it consecrated and blessed,' Sumdar replied, his gaze fixed on the thangka. 'I've dedicated the twilight of my life to this precious painting. I need to have it blessed by the Precious Lama.' Lama Ngawang Chogyal was the fifteenth abbot of Ralung revered as Drukchen or Great Drukpa Ngawang Chogyal.

'Hmm, not a bad idea,' said the cocky man.

As Sumdar squatted, frozen in deep appreciation of the thangka, a forceful torrent of water splashed on it. The yellowish stream crashed on the central figure and the droplets bouncing off it jumped about and rolled over other images across the thangka before the devout owner could react.

'Goodness gracious!' cried Sumdar, seeing the Tibetan man furiously urinating on his thangka. 'What are you doing, you lunatic mendicant?'

He broke down. He protested, but words dissolved into his quivering voice. He was on all fours, teary and lost, pale and trembling.

The Tibetan man rolled up the dripping wet thangka and handed it to Sumdar. 'Now take it to your lama,' he said calmly, walking away with his dog following him.

Sumdar was left behind holding the stinky wet thangka. He had trudged for days across treacherous mountains, sleeping rough and eating little. His exhausted body had turned limp.

His only precious possession had been desecrated in the worst possible way.

After a long while, the broken man gathered himself. The precious thangka now looked like a bundle of rags to him. Yet, he hoped that his lama would redeem his misfortune.

After several days, Sumdar presented himself before Lama Ngawang Chogyal in Ralung and recounted his encounter with the strange Tibetan wanderer who had desecrated his thangka.

As he unfurled the thangka before the lama, it glittered softly. It had turned golden. Every place the urine had touched was awash with gold.

After looking at the thangka long and hard, the lama shook his head in quiet wonderment and declared, 'Your thangka doesn't need any consecration. It's been blessed by Drukpa Kunley, who has urinated gold on it.'

CHAPTER 12

When a Wanderer Meets a Treasure Revealer[52]

---

52 In Tibetan Buddhism, a **treasure revealer**, or *terton*, is a person believed to be destined and, therefore, have the spiritual ability to discover hidden teachings or sacred objects known as *terma*. *Terma* are teachings or artifacts that were hidden centuries ago by enlightened beings, such as Padmasambhava. These treasures are destined to be discovered and shared with future generations when the teachings are most needed.

One day, Drukpa Kunley was journeying along the ancient trail of Monla Karchung, the mountain pass between Bumthang and Tibet. He wished to go straight to Kurje, where the great saint Padmasambhava had meditated and left the imprint of his body in a cave in the eighth century. Near the cave stood a giant cypress tree believed to have grown from Padmasambhava's walking staff. Some distance from the cave flowed a small holy spring.

He walked slowly and meditatively, admiring the mesmerizing landscapes of Bumthang, the spiritual heartland of Bhutan. He felt underdressed but savoured the cold alpine air, crisp and invigorating, scented with pine and prayer.

Before him spread broad valleys, gentle hills and sparkling streams. The houses with slanting wooden roofs were elegant and beautiful. Small bamboo and cane dwellings were inviting like peaceful hermitages. All kinds of medicinal herbs, flowers and fruits adorned the valleys. He paused to take a deep, meditative breath with great satisfaction.

The beauty of the land reminded him of the great Tibetan saint Kunkhyen Longchen Rabjam (1308–1364), popularly known as Longchenpa, who had traversed the sacred region of Bumthang a century earlier and described it as a heavenly hidden abode with unparalleled beauty. Longchenpa's legacy flourished at the time in the form of many monasteries and temples strewn over hills and vales.

Before crossing into Bhutan, Drukpa Kunley had visited some of Tibet's most sacred Buddhist sites, such as Drowolung Monastery, the seat of Marpa the Translator (1012–1097), and Sekhar Guthog, the nine-storey monument built by his principal disciple, the great yogi Milarepa (1052–1135). But never had he felt so euphoric with boundless spiritual energy that pervaded him in Bumthang.

Word of Drukpa Kunley's arrival in Bumthang quickly spread across the villages. As soon as he reached Kurje, the girls of Bumthang, with their heads wrapped in a piece of cloth, flocked to meet him with chang, devotion and desire.

'Naljorpa, we have come to meet you to establish spiritual and sexual connections with you,' they said. 'All right, we will establish both the connections,' Drukpa Kunley said, sitting amid beautiful girls. He drank all their chang and slept with many of them. He remarked that he had never met girls with softer skin and better sexual prowess than the girls of Mon.

One morning, as Drukpa Kunley met his devotees, he shared with them a curious revelation. As someone accustomed to urinating in the open, he found himself unable to find even a small patch of ground around Kurje where he could answer the call of nature. This was because every blade of grass bore the sacred letter 'ah' (ཨ). He did not want to desecrate the sacred letter and consequently all good and sacred things originating from it.

In Buddhism, 'ah', the last of the thirty letters of the Tibetan alphabet, is considered 'the supreme of all letters'[53]. It is unborn and self-arisen, hence considered the source of all other letters. 'Ah' is the most powerful syllable for incantation, with most commonly chanted mantras beginning with it or its variants.

When combined with other letters, 'ah' forms words that convey the finest of human qualities such as love, affection, respect and leadership. For example, apa for father, ama for mother, azhang and akhu for uncle, ani for aunt, acho for elder brother, azhem for elder sister, alu for child, angay for grandmother, agay for grandfather and azhe for queen or princess, all begin with the letter 'ah'.

---

53 ཨ་ནི་ཡིག་འབྲུ་ཀུན་གྱི་མཆོག

Drukpa Kunley's presence in Bumthang did not go unnoticed by Chagkhar Gyalpo, the powerful king of Chagkhar or the Iron Castle, who suspected that he was a bogus yogi. The first Chagkhar Gyalpo Sindhu Raja was believed to have been an Indian prince who had settled in Bumthang on a self-imposed exile after a battle with another Indian prince called Nawoche. He was credited for inviting Padmasambhava to Bhutan in the eighth century, bringing the light of Buddhism to the country for the first time.

One evening, the king invited Drukpa Kunley and three of his attendant monks to a single-storey house with a black flag on the roof. The house was eerily silent with only a lone woman inside. She placed food and a gourd bottle of chang before them, then turned her back on them without a word. They ate all the food and emptied the chang bottle.

The following morning, as Drukpa Kunley and his monks emerged from the house, they came across two Tibetan yogis in a stone enclosure. One lay dead, the other barely clinging to life. The survivor rasped that they had been served food and drink by a lone woman in a single-storey house with a black flag on the roof. He said she was a poisoner. The king had ordered the same woman to poison Drukpa Kunley and his monks with her food and drink to test Drukpa Kunley's authenticity. But the poison had no effect on them.

When they returned to the king's castle, the rogue courtiers of the king launched a surprise attack, shooting poisoned arrows and darts laced with deadly toxins. Drukpa Kunley, unfazed, swatted them aside like flies. Then, he brought the king tumbling down from his throne. 'Will you listen to me now?' he boomed. 'If not, I will dispatch you.' The king and his courtiers were humiliated and humbled. 'You are an unmistakable adept,' they said, bowing low before Drukpa Kunley with deep reverence.

Drukpa Kunley now felt accepted in Bumthang. He wanted to leave something behind for the locals for all the good chang and devotion he had been offered. He built a small temple called Monsib Lhakhang, appointed a resident lama, and enrolled thirty people as monks. Then, he gave the locals instructions on mani and badza guru, the mantra of Padmasambhava.

Before he departed, he said to a group of devotees, 'I've not come here looking for the girls of Lhomon because I'm sexually starved. I've had to display some miracles, although I have little accomplishment. I've had to do something to make the occasion auspicious, although my service to the dharma is anything but substantial. I've not come here in search of food and clothes either, for I've left behind all the offerings I've received.'

Drukpa Kunley left Kurje in search of the Dharma Lord of Bumthang, Terton Pema Lingpa, who was the fourth of the five king treasure revealers and the foremost spiritual figure native to Bhutan. Terton Pema Lingpa was a blacksmith, mason, carpenter, teacher, yogi and treasure revealer—all at once. He was believed to have been the reincarnation of Longchenpa. It was as if Longchenpa had returned to Bumthang, the place he was fascinated with, to continue his spiritual activities.

Drukpa Kunley found Terton Pema Lingpa in a marketplace, teaching a group of people from a high throne. Terton Pema Lingpa was of average build. Despite his exalted status, he appeared unassuming, clad in simple attire that blended seamlessly with the crowd.

Nearby, Drukpa Kunley playfully gathered a troupe of children around him and mounting a boulder, began mimicking the actions of the revered treasure revealer. The distracted crowd looked askance at Drukpa Kunley and the children around him, who seemed to be enjoying themselves. As the mimicry continued for a while, Terton Pema Lingpa turned to Drukpa Kunley and said dismissively, 'I'm teaching the views, meditation, and actions of Dzogchen[54] here. What is the meaning of this, beggar?' Drukpa Kunley turned away from the children and sang this song that echoed the essence of the view and meditation of Dzogchen.

> High and lofty may be Mount Kailash
> Yet, the snow lion must thrive on its own.
> Deep and vast may be Dzogchen's vision
> Yet, seekers must find the mind's nature on their own.
> Boundless, vast and deep may be the ocean
> Yet, fish must navigate its depths on their own.
> Profound may be the conceptions of Sutras
> Yet, practitioners must learn to meditate on their own.
> Tertons may have numerous spiritual consorts
> But monks find pleasure in more loving wives.
> Stringent and orderly may Vinaya's conduct look
> But the Great Perfection is more inward-looking.

Terton Pema Lingpa was pleasantly surprised by Drukpa Kunley's meaningful song. 'This fellow is not a beggar,' he concluded. He said this in response.

---

54 Great Perfection, an ancient teaching believed to be at the heart of all teachings of the Buddha and traced back to Dharmakaya Samantabhadra.

> The so-called view is viewless in essence
> And beyond existence and non-existence.
> How can it be seen when sought after?
> If it can be seen, then it is not the view.
> The profound act of meditation
> Transcends all points of reference.
> There is no meditation where there are references,
> Where references persist, there is no meditation.
> Conduct involving acceptance and rejection
> Transcends the bounds of acceptance and rejection.
> With acceptance and rejection, there is no conduct,
> Without them, can there be virtues and vices?

Drukpa Kunley smiled and nodded affirmatively. He said as long as compassion was born from meditation, there was no such thing as good or bad conduct.

In a gesture of reverence, Terton Pema Lingpa took off his hat and said, 'You are truly remarkable. Pray tell, from which illustrious lineage do you hail? What teachings have you received, and how have you diligently practised them?'

Drukpa Kunley introduced his lineage, his revered lamas, the teachings he had received from them, and practices dear to him. Among his cherished practices, he emphasized the conscious cultivation of love for others above self.

After their conversation drifted from lofty philosophical musings to intimate exchanges, mutual respect blossomed, forging a special bond of friendship transcending geographical and cultural boundaries. The next few days they spent together marked the highlight of Drukpa Kunley's sojourn in Bumthang.

Drukpa Kunley and Terton Pema Lingpa would have a few encounters later on, which were not as pleasant as these few days.

On one occasion, Terton Pema Lingpa was at the centre of a controversy. He endorsed the second reincarnation of Tibetan saint Dorji Lingpa (1346–1405), Chogden Gonpo, despite a dispute over his claim in Tibet, where he was born. Drukpa Kunley, who happened to be around, challenged Chogden Gonpo to a contest of miracles to establish the authenticity of his claim. Terton Pema Lingpa immediately sprung to Chogden Gonpo's defence saying any such contest must be between him and Drukpa Kunley since the reincarnate lama was still a child. For once, Drukpa Kunley was humbled.

On another occasion, Terton Pema Lingpa offered his interpretation of these enigmatic lines, 'I, Samantabhadra, am the Buddha. I, Samantabhadra, am the hell.'[55] He said, 'Clouds can disappear, but the sky will endure. Similarly, discursive thought can disappear, but the spontaneously arisen wisdom will endure.'

Drukpa Kunley, renowned for his unorthodox insights, contested Terton Pema Lingpa's interpretation, asserting that the lines underlined the unity underlying diverse manifestations. 'This is what these lines mean,' he said. 'Although phenomena assume different forms, in essence, they are one and the same. For example, if I go to war, I would be called General Kunley. If I sing, I would be called Singer Kunley. And if I teach, I would be known as Choje Kunley. But in essence, there is only one Kunley.'

Terton Pema Lingpa humbly acknowledged the alternative interpretation of the lines. He said, 'I do not have a lama, and I did not undergo rigorous training to gain scholarship. Whatever I have achieved must be appreciated.'

CHAPTER 13

If You Persist, Even Your Mother Relents

'What's become of your life, Kunley?' chided his mother. 'If you claim to be a religious person, you should be working for the welfare of sentient beings. If you are now a layman, it's time you brought home a wife who will help your ageing mother.'

Drukpa Kunley was back home in Ralung. He sat by the fireplace, deep in thought. He was contemplating practising and teaching the dharma as a carefree itinerant. He had left the monastic community upon realizing that enlightenment did not depend on scriptural erudition or righteous moral conduct. He concluded that no external factor could liberate a person without recognizing the buddha within.

'Do you know where your life is headed?' continued his mother. 'You cannot be neither religious nor lay.'

Drukpa Kunley listened to his mother's chiding with calm nonchalance and a knowing smile. 'It may be time to teach and awaken whomever I come across through crazy wisdom,' he thought. He knew his mother must be purged of her judgmental perceptions and prejudices.

Still smiling, he sprang up with alacrity, saying, 'If you want me to bring home a wife, I can do that immediately.' His mother was surprised at the way he brushed aside her serious admonition with a smile.

In minutes, Drukpa Kunley was in the marketplace of Ralung, standing before a hundred-year-old lady, grey-haired, toothless and stooping. He carried her home and presented her before his mother. 'Here's she, my wife, to fulfil your wish,' he said.

'What a shame,' whined his mother. 'Kunley, if this is all you can bring home, I can perform your wife's duty. Now take her back.'

At that time, Lama Ngawang Chogyal, the exalted manifestation of the Bodhisattva of Compassion, was undergoing two-stage meditation. He strictly refrained from all immodest and shameful behaviours.

Drukpa Kunley picked up the old lady and put her on his back. 'If that's what you are willing to perform—a wife's duty—I will take her back,' he said, striding out.

Meanwhile, Lama Ngawang Chogyal took a short break from meditation and thought that their house needed renovation. He told himself that a religious household must have a shrine room. An indoor toilet is indispensable when someone is in a strict retreat, so, a toilet needed to be built too.

When Drukpa Kunley returned from the marketplace, Lama Ngawang Chogyal was struggling to find the right location for the toilet. 'The eastern side of the house is not suitable,' he thought. 'The southern side is aesthetically not pleasing. The western side is not even worth considering.'

As Drukpa Kunley walked into his home, his mother resumed her chiding. 'Listen, Kunley,' she said, 'a good son should be like Ngawang Chogyal. He serves his lama and parents well, works tirelessly for the welfare of sentient beings, and looks after his own spiritual growth.'

Drukpa Kunley looked at his mother and chuckled heartily. His mother did not find that funny. She raised her voice and continued her efforts to draw an answer from him, 'Kunley, do you see what he does for others and himself?'

'You do not know,' Drukpa Kunley cut in, 'the agony your exemplary son is going through trying to find a suitable location for the toilet he is planning to build.'

That night, Drukpa Kunley crept near his mother's bed and lay beside her.

'What are you doing here, Kunley?' asked his mother.

'This morning, you said you could perform a wife's duty for me,' he said.

'Now don't be stupid and shameless,' she rebuked him sharply, sitting up in bed. 'I meant I could do household chores.'

'You should have said it that way,' he said. 'Now, I have to sleep with you.'

'This is utterly repugnant, you incorrigible brat,' she protested. 'Go back to your bed before the whole town starts talking about this.'

'If you are so stubborn, our relationship ends here,' Drukpa Kunley said in all seriousness.

'Kunley, your dogged persistence is sickening,' his mother said. 'Now, shut up and go away.'

But Drukpa Kunley did not budge from her bedside. Feigning a crippling pain in his knees, he refused to go back to his bed. After persistent nagging for a long time, his mother relented. 'Come now, make sure no one knows about it,' she said.

Hurray! Drukpa Kunley jumped to his feet gleefully and disappeared. He had waited for his mother to say that. The words jarred and crackled in his ears.

The following morning, he went straight to the marketplace and announced, 'Listen up, folks! If you persist, even your mother relents.'

As Drukpa Kunley walked away, everybody exclaimed in disbelief, 'What's become of Drukpa Kunley!'

The great shame Drukpa Kunley brought to his mother cleansed her of all her sins. She lived a long, one hundred and thirty years of blessed and healthy life.

CHAPTER 14
Philandering Nuns' Paternity Claim Refuted

PHILANDERING NUNS' PATERNITY CLAIM REFUTED

One day the young nuns of Ralung were in a salacious mood. They gathered in their hostel and laughed with gay abandon. They slapped one another on their clean-shaven heads, saying, 'It's your turn now. Go find your Drukpa Kunley.'

Their friend Ani Tshewang Palzom, from the nunnery, had given birth to an extraordinary boy and declared Drukpa Kunley as the child's father. Lama Ngawang Chogyal, the stern abbot of the nunnery, had surprisingly cleared her of sexual misconduct. 'Drukpa Kunley is a madman, so Tshewang can't be blamed for this moral aberration,' he had said.

Nine months ago, Drukpa Kunley was on his way to Ralung from Tsang when he came across Ani Tshewang Palzom, who was on her alms round in the village. Swathed in clean maroon robes, she looked beautiful with a radiant smile. As she stepped aside, Drukpa Kunley stood before her and said in his typically unconventional and direct style, 'Ani, you are just ripe and too charming for a nun. Let's do it.'

She blushed and said she was a nun unschooled in the ways of the sensual world. 'You don't have to be skillful at this,' Drukpa Kunley said with a charming smile. 'I will give it a good rhythm.' As she stepped back, his hands were already on her. He pulled her beside the footpath and climaxed on her three times at a go, which resulted in her pregnancy.

'It's our turn now. Let's go find our Drukpa Kunley,' the young nuns said to one another, giggling.

'But we are nuns, and we are expected to remain chaste,' one of them said, sounding cautious. 'Besides, our lama will not spare us if we went out with men and came back with babies.'

'For girls our age, nothing is more gratifying than sex,' another said. 'If we say Drukpa Kunley is the father of the baby, we will be forgiven like Tshewang. Here's our opportunity to discover the most pleasurable thing in the world.'

'So, let's go find our Drukpa Kunley,' others chimed in unison.

Nine months later, one of the nuns gave birth, followed by another and six others. Soon, eight nuns from the nunnery had had babies. Each of them claimed that Drukpa Kunley was the father of their baby. The whole of Tibet started talking about Ralung's nunnery, Drukpa Kunley, and Lama Ngawang Chogyal. The word spread that the mad Drukpa had impregnated all the Ralung nuns, and the nunnery had turned into a birthing centre.

Lama Ngawang Chogyal was extremely distraught. His nunnery, which had enjoyed a good reputation for its academic rigour, had suddenly become the laughing stock of the whole nation. He hung his head in shame. 'This is intolerable!' he fumed. 'Kunley has thoroughly tarnished the nunnery's and my reputation. I thought he wouldn't repeat his behaviour after the incident involving Ani Tshewang Palzom.'

However, he could do nothing to salvage his reputation of an accomplished lama, especially with Drukpa Kunley nowhere to be found around Ralung. Drukpa Kunley was constantly on the move and rarely stayed in Ralung. No one knew how soon he would return to Ralung to answer his cousin regarding his disgraceful behaviour.

Before long, Drukpa Kunley learnt what was happening in Ralung. Although he had no reputation to protect or salvage, he returned to Ralung and summoned all the nuns who had claimed that he was their child's father. Nine of them, including Ani Tshewang Palzom, came to meet Drukpa Kunley with their children.

'They could all be my babies,' Drukpa Kunley told them, 'but I need to check if they are really mine.'

'Look, my child's face looks exactly like yours,' claimed one of them. Drukpa Kunley looked at the child's face and smiled.

'Look, my child's hands resemble yours,' claimed another.

'My child's legs are no different from yours,' said the third nun. Drukpa Kunley kept quiet with a sardonic smile.

'Look at his eyes,' said the fourth nun, pointing at her baby. 'They are the spitting image of your eyes.'

'Now look at this,' the fifth nun cut in. 'My baby's nose is indistinguishable from yours.'

Ani Tshewang Palzom stood quietly and demurely, tenderly cradling her child, who would grow up to become the famous son of Drukpa Kunley, Zhingchong Drukdra. She neither said anything nor reacted to all the outlandish claims.

Drukpa Kunley lowered his bow, planted it on the ground like a walking staff, and said, 'Well, well, well. They could all be my babies. But I need to check if they are really mine.' Then, he held Ani Tshewang Palzom's baby by the legs and chanted:

> Hearken, Palden Lhamo, the bearer of Wisdom Eyes.
> I, Druk Nyon Kunley, who roam the vast land
> May have slept with a string of young girls,
> But I am being tricked by these lying nuns.
> If he is my son, catch him with your hands,
> If he is not, dispatch him with your mouth.

Saying so, he swung the baby over his head and tossed him into the air. The baby safely landed in the middle of an empty field with a resounding thud accompanied by a thunderclap. Alarmed by the scene, the philandering nuns took flight in fright and shame, carrying their babies.

CHAPTER 15
Beyond Dress and Appearance

'Your manner of dress is neither a lama's, nor a monk's, and not even a yogi's,' a senior geshe[56] said to Drukpa Kunley. 'Yours is a medley of different pieces that don't belong to any spiritual practitioner.'

Drukpa Kunley was in the fortress of Jayul's governor, Onsa Chogyal Lingpa. He was half drunk and engaged in a jovial conversation with a group of geshes, gomchens[57] and monks. The geshes were dressed in a full set of yellow and maroon robes, with their heads shaven clean. The gomchens wore white inner gowns, maroon robes and long hair. The monks wore fully maroon robes without yellow frills. Everybody talked softly.

'You set a bad example for lay people,' the geshe continued in a respectful tone.

Everybody looked at Drukpa Kunley, anticipating a maverick reaction from him. But Drukpa Kunley was not bothered at all. He simply nodded as if in agreement and smiled broadly.

'Why don't you settle down somewhere instead of roaming like a dog aimlessly?' asked the geshe.

Drukpa Kunley did not seem eager to answer him. He took a sip of chang and relished it as if chang mattered to him more than the geshe's provocative question. He had reflected on the question that the geshe was asking numerous times before he began his peripatetic life, and he had all the answers.

'The answer to your question is not easy,' Drukpa Kunley said. 'To be a monk, I have to follow all the monastic vows, which is

---

56 Buddhist scholar holding the highest degree in Tibet.
57 Hermit or meditator. Today, people practicing dharma part-time in lay clothing are also known as *gomchens*.

difficult in this age of five degenerations[58]. There is nothing more nauseating than monks without moral discipline. To be a yogi, I have to realize the nature of the mind, which is not tangible and graspable. Someone pretending to be a yogi is like a donkey in a leopard's skin.'

Everyone nodded in agreement.

'If I were a lama,' he continued, putting down his cup and looking at it, 'I would be obliged to serve my disciples. Hence, I would lose my freedom.'

His tone was more contemplative than argumentative. He seemed to talk to himself rather than in response to the geshe's question. The geshes listened to him intently and nodded.

He took another sip of chang and put the cup down. His chang, served from a wooden container, was slightly cloudy and frothy with a sharp, citric flavour. Every sip was pungent and heady. He smacked his lips and continued, 'Whether my behaviour sets a bad example for lay people will depend on how discerning they are. I see people whose actions are as wholesome as Lord Buddha descending into hell. I think buddhahood is not impossible for those with an idiosyncratic appearance or manner of dress.'

'Hmm, this rings true,' one of the geshes observed. 'You are right, Drukpa.' Others agreed, 'He is right.'

Drukpa Kunley said that staying in one place for a long time was detrimental to spiritual growth. It reinforced the sense of settling down and belonging to a place which, in turn, created a false sense of permanence. 'Trivial differences in the respect one receives give rise to attachment and aversion stronger than

---

58 སྙིགས་མ་ལྔ་ : The degeneration of the eon, the degeneration of afflictions, the degeneration of beings, the degeneration of views, and the degeneration of lifespan.

lay people's,' he said. 'A religious establishment is started for the dharma, but it has to be managed with adroitness and craft, making monastic life more chaotic than the mundane world.'

'You are right, Drukpa,' the geshes said. 'Thank you. Now, please share with us the spiritual commitments dear to you.'

Drukpa Kunley paused to gather his thoughts. He picked up his cup and drank deep from it as though the chang contained all his spiritual commitments. Then he knitted his brow, cupped his chin in his left palm, and looked at the chang container before him.

'You may not be able to do big things,' he said, 'but it is important to stay committed to doing essential things.' Then he sang:

> I may not be able to pray wholeheartedly
> To the Triple Gem, the sole refuge of all beings.
> Yet, I vow to uphold the three-line refuge prayer.
> Hold this vow dear to your heart, my friends.
>
> I may not exchange my comfort wholeheartedly
> With others' misery in the spirit of bodhichitta.
> Yet, I vow not to be swayed by selfish desires.
> Hold this vow dear to your heart, my friends.
>
> I may not be able to propitiate appropriately
> The deities who bear blessings in varied forms.
> Yet, I vow not to tread the path of black magic.
> Hold this vow dear to your heart, my friends.
>
> I may not be able to appease guardian deities,
> The destroyers of enemies, with ritual offerings.

Yet, I vow not to disparage my enemies like dogs.
Hold this vow dear to your heart, my friends.

I may not be able to meditate without references
And with devotion on the primordially pure view.
Yet, I vow not to hold on to only substance and attributes.
Hold this vow dear to your heart, my friends.

I may not be able to experience the stream of reality
In the meditative equipoise that is luminous like the sky.
Yet, I vow not to quit my regular meditative sessions.
Hold this vow dear to your heart, my friends.

I may not have grasped the full extent and fruition
Of renunciation and realization within my being.
Yet, I vow not to be impatient for it in the future.
Hold this vow dear to your heart, my friends.

I may not be able to practise with unfettered ease
The dharma that's beyond speech, thought and utterance.
Yet, I vow not to cling to fabricated mental conceptions.
Hold this vow dear to your heart, my friends.

As Drukpa Kunley continued his exposition on spiritual commitments essential to leading a virtuous life, the host and geshes were moved to appreciation and veneration for his profound wisdom. They joined their palms and thanked him.

As he stood up to leave, he added, 'I may not be able to live up to the rigour of a disciplined life, but I'm committed to not hiding behind the veneer of hypocrisy and duplicity. The dharma is beyond manner of dress.'

BEYOND DRESS AND APPEARANCE || 87

Drukpa Kunley returned to Jayul after a few months, drawn by a feast offering ceremony taking place atop the governor's fortress. He found himself amid a crowd of Drukpa tent dwellers, intoxicated and singing. The governor seemed cheerful and jubilant. They offered Drukpa Kunley copious amounts of chang and requested him to sing a delightful song. Drukpa Kunley sang this song celebrating the life of a carefree wanderer.

> Gladly I'm not a common lama,
> For if I were, worshipped by all;
> Seeking followers and offerings,
> I wouldn't find time for the dharma.
>
> Gladly I'm not a monastic monk,
> For if I were, amidst the crowd;
> Chasing after novice monks for love,
> There's no time for Sutras and Tantras.
>
> Gladly I do not dwell in a hermitage,
> For if I did, high up in the mountains;
> The radiant smile of attendant ladies
> Leaves no room for the Three Vows.
>
> Gladly I'm not a tantric magician,
> For if I were, wielding dark power;
> Cutting others' lives thin and short
> Leaves no goodness for bodhichitta.

Gladly I'm not a Chod[59] practitioner,
For if I were, yelling a series of phet[60];
Confronting gods and evil spirits
Leaves no time to slay afflictions.

Gladly I do not live with my family,
For if I did, immersed in their midst;
Distressed by the daily grind for survival,
There's no spirit for carefree wanderings.

As Drukpa Kunley ended his song, the intoxicated monks rose from their seats, applauding him boisterously. 'Wonderful, Drukpa Kunley!' they exclaimed. 'The governor's chang is a feast for the mouth, but your song is a feast for the ears.'

Then, Drukpa Kunley emptied his chang cup and rose to leave, saying, 'I must get going. You all are dwellers but I'm a wanderer. If I linger any longer here, I might get attached to the opulence of the palace or the warmth of your friendly gestures.' And with that, he turned and disappeared into the night, alone and carefree once again.

---

59 Literally 'cut', it is a system of practices based on Prajnaparamita introduced by the Indian siddha Phadampa Sangye and the Tibetan female teacher Machig Labdron for the purpose of cutting through the four Maras and ego-clinging.

60 The syllable is a Sanskrit metaphor for 'cutting through' and central to the Chod ritual.

CHAPTER 16

No Virtuous Abbot for Dechenphu

Drukpa Kunley was back at the Ralung Monastery after many years. He had been summoned by the abbot there. Having forsaken the monastic life to roam as a wanderer, Drukpa Kunley rarely visited Ralung or heeded the directives of the abbot.

Located in the Tsang region of western Tibet, Ralung Monastery was founded in 1180 by Tsangpa Gyare, the founding father of the Drukpa Kagyu school of Buddhism. The monastery was located in a wide valley fringed by lofty, barren mountains. It was Drukpa Kunley's ancestral and spiritual home. Yet, as a carefree wanderer, he rarely felt attached to it. In fact, he practised remaining detached from all monastic establishments, including Ralung.

Warm greetings were exchanged as he presented himself before the abbot inside the imposing monastery. The abbot, whom he respectfully addressed as the Precious Lord of Ralung, seated on an ornate throne, proposed, 'Kunley, since you have no intention of returning to Ralung, why don't you look after Dechenbu[61] Monastery in the southern country of Mon?' The abbot sat on a high throne and Drukpa Kunley sat cross-legged on a small mat before the throne. An attendant tiptoed in with a teapot.

'I cannot accept that responsibility as I have no desire to settle permanently in Mon,' submitted Drukpa Kunley matter-of-factly.

'You do not have to live there permanently,' the abbot said, wiping his wooden cup with a piece of cloth and placing it on the

---

61 ནོ་བདེ་ཆེན་ཕུག： Lopon Kunzang Thinley, the editor-in-chief of KMT Publishing House and a foremost Bhutan scholar, says this is an old Tibetan variant of Dechenphu (spelt བདེ་ཆེན་ཕུག or བདེ་ཆེན་ཕུ་) in Thimphu. As the abode of Drukpa dharma protector Geynyen Jagpa Melen, Dechenphu had been popular in Ralung since its first abbot, Onrey Dharma Singye (1177-1237).

right corner of the table before him. 'You can appoint someone virtuous and go there occasionally.'

'Someone virtuous?' Drukpa Kunley asked. 'Kindly find him yourself, Lord. For me, finding someone virtuous is like the paradox of building an irrigation channel across a sand dune that Tsangpa Gyare spoke of.'

'This is even more difficult, because in order to manage a monastery and care for disciples, one has to be avaricious enough to gather and keep things even as small as needles and threads. While at the same time, generous enough to relinquish everything.'

Meanwhile, the attendant filled the abbot's cup. The abbot picked up the steaming cup and placed it before him.

As the attendant knelt before him to serve tea, Drukpa Kunley elucidated further, 'You need someone disciplined enough to renounce others' wealth like poison and perseverant enough to mind his own smell, and not bother about others'. You need someone tolerant enough to stand a beating even by nuns and with a sharp meditative concentration that puts off thoughts about others for later.'

The attendant poured a steaming cup of tea as Drukpa Kunley continued, 'To manage a monastery and care for disciples, you need someone with wisdom to understand the present and future interests of both spiritual and temporal affairs; someone with wisdom to get along even with children, but in a desperate situation, unafraid to stand up even to the Lord of Death.'

As the abbot chanted the tea offering verse, picking up his cup, Drukpa Kunley chanted along. As the two took the first few sips of tea, silence returned to the abbot's chamber, which was adorned with colourful murals and brocade thangkas. The murals depicted, among others, the saints of the Kagyu lineage and Atisha Dipamkara (982–1054), the great saint from Bengal credited for playing a crucial role in reviving Buddhism in Tibet after a period of persecution.

'Are you saying nobody has the virtues you have described?' asked the abbot. 'I thought you would consider my proposition.'

'No,' replied Drukpa Kunley, 'I'm not saying nobody has such virtues, but people with such virtues are rare and hard to find. Moreover, you need someone diligent enough to earn his own food, clothes and people's regard while being detached enough to remain content even without any of them. You need someone large-hearted and calm, noble and cautious; someone whose speech is more pleasant than a cat's mew, but whose core nature is harder to twist than an old yak's neck. You need someone who can examine any person he comes across and after examining his or her virtues and vices, cannot be swayed by anyone.

'You need someone who does not cut ties with his relatives and friends while at the same time is not partial towards them; someone who does not dismiss the instructions of genuine masters while not falling prey to deceitful teachers; someone whose short-term actions correspond with how other people treat him but who recognizes the principle of cause and action and that bad actions lead one to the lower realms; someone who does not proclaim his virtuous deeds while guarding his good conduct at the same time; someone who never forgets, now and always, that good begets good and evil begets evil; someone who speaks less, but is capable of a stream of words with correct usage and meaning when situations demand.'

'Just like you do right now because you don't want to go south, isn't it?' remarked the abbot, smiling broadly.

'Gift of the gab is not even my virtue,' Drukpa Kunley said. 'My best virtues are the ones that I do not have rather than those that I have, including not having any future plans and not harbouring evil thoughts for others. But here, I'm talking about the virtues one must have to manage a monastery and care for disciples. You need someone who has the humility to bow before the enemy he cannot defeat and a good heart to desist from being wicked and vindictive when you can defeat the enemy; someone who can fathom the contexts and limits of all religious and secular activities; someone who does not flaunt his strength and bravery; someone who treats everyone fairly and can distinguish those who serve from those who harm.'

'To manage a monastery and care for disciples,' Drukpa Kunley continued, 'you need someone who understands the limits of straight talk and lies in all kinds of engagements; someone who understands that except for the omniscient Buddha, nothing ultimately helps; someone who does not trust anything that is not in harmony with what the Buddha has taught; someone who can tell true dharma practitioners from charlatans after scrutinizing whether they love others more than themselves.'

The abbot was enthralled by Drukpa Kunley's spontaneous and lucid exposition of virtues a monastic leader must have. It was partly spiritual wisdom, partly worldly sagacity. He had never listened to such an exposition and felt quite odd listening to Drukpa Kunley from his high throne. He leant forward and nodded intermittently.

Drukpa Kunley paused to look into his cup. There was only some tea left. He emptied the cup to the lees before rising to take leave. Standing, with the cup in his hand, he expressed his final thoughts, 'Precious Lord, such a person is indeed virtuous. I'm not sure if such a person would want to be my servant. However precious coral is, it can be likened to a person without these virtues. Someone with these qualities has to be a jewel instead. A virtuous person will lead many people to happiness, whereas a person without virtues will lead many to disgrace.'

And as the abbot watched him disappear, his footsteps echoing across the corridor, a sense of reverence filled his heart. For in that fleeting moment, he had glimpsed the true essence of virtuous leadership in the form of Drukpa Kunley—who refused to be a leader.

CHAPTER 17

Wager Not Your Fish Away

Tired, exasperated and hopeless, Nyapa[62] Tshering slumped heavily on the floor. He had just returned from Yamdro lake, where he had gone fishing with other men from his village, Gadra, in the Yamdro province of Tibet. 'Not even a needle-sized one,' he told his wife, hurling his grimy cloth bag into a corner.

Dusk was descending on the village. It had been more than a month since the last time that the men from Gadra had succeeded in hooking or netting any fish from the lake that had provided food for generations of the Gadrawa, the people of Gadra. The whole village was famished. The proud men looked woebegone. The children whined in hunger. The women launched furious tirades at their husbands and called them weaklings.

As night fell on the hungry village, some people came knocking at Nyapa Tshering's door to discuss how to save themselves from starvation. One of them said, 'The fish are gone. We're dying. We must go to Druk Nyon Kunga Legpa posthaste and request him to withdraw his order for Lady Mermaid.'

Everybody nodded in agreement. A flickering oil lamp sat near Nyapa Tshering.

More than a month ago, the same group had gathered at Nyapa Tshering's house to eat and drink as usual. They feasted on a mountain of fish, and drank like fish. They belched noisily, talked boisterously, and roared with laughter. Some monks had joined them in the feast.

As the group turned rowdy and bawdy, with men throwing half-chewed fish at women to attract their attention, Drukpa Kunley, known to Gadrawa as Druk Nyon Kunga Legpa, barged in.

---

[62] Fisherman

Some acknowledged the wanderer's arrival and showed him a place to sit, but most did not even glance at him. Drukpa Kunley put down his bow and quiver and made room for himself in a corner. His long hair was tied into a loose bundle behind his head, and large silver-coloured rings dangled from his ears. He quickly gulped down a few cups of chang and joined the boisterous conversation that skimmed over numerous topics, including fishing, hunting and killing.

When the conversation settled on archery, the villagers challenged Drukpa Kunley and his monks to a game of archery. 'If we win, we take your silk clothes and horses. If you win, you can harvest our crop,' they challenged. Drukpa Kunley said he had no silk clothes and horses and was not interested in taking up the challenge. However, the monks had silk clothes and horses, so the confident villagers insisted and Drukpa Kunley relented.

The match began. The Gadrawas gathered fifteen of their best archers against Drukpa Kunley and fourteen monks. The monks, led by Drukpa Kunley, pulverized the villagers in three straight games.

The villagers, shaken and ashamed, gathered around Drukpa Kunley with gold coins, large quantities of meat and chang, and proposed, 'Let this be what you have earned with your victory.' But Drukpa Kunley insisted that his team would only take the wager the villagers had offered.

The villagers broke into raucous laughter, thinking Drukpa Kunley was declining tangible things they were offering him and demanding something he could never have. 'Take it then. We survive on fish from Yamdro Lake. Harvest our crop from the lake as much as you wish,' the villagers said.

'All right,' Drukpa Kunley said. 'We will.'

Taking a piece of paper and a bamboo pen, he wrote a letter to Lady Mermaid of Yamdro lake. Yamdro was one of the largest and most sacred lakes in Tibet. It was believed to have been created by Khandro Yeshe Tshogyal—the principal consort of Padmasambhava—by combining nine smaller lakes.

Someone on a horseback pilgrimage was said to typically take one whole month to go around it once. But a classical Bhutanese song goes, 'The turquoise lake of Yamdro in Tibet/Is eighteen days for a horse.'[63] This lyric suggests that it takes eighteen days to go around it once on horseback. Its turquoise water was thick with fish.

'I've won from the people of Gadra the life-sustaining fish from your lake in an archery match,' the letter read. 'From today onwards, let no fish—those as big as a sheep or as tiny as a needle—swim in your lake until I instruct you otherwise. Issued on the twenty-seventh day of the fifth lunar month of the Dog Year.'

Drukpa Kunley threw the letter into the lake. Starting that day, Nyapa Tshering and other men from Gadra could not catch a single fish from the lake.

'Yes, we must go back to Druk Nyon Kunga Legpa,' Nyapa Tshering said authoritatively, adding oil to the flickering lamp. Everybody nodded in agreement once again.

They went to see Drukpa Kunley with a lot of meat and chang. 'Please do not starve us to death,' they pleaded with him.

'I'm now caught in an odd situation,' Drukpa Kunley said. But he took his pen and paper and wrote a letter to the Lord of Death.

The letter read: 'I'm pleased with the tidings of your exacting judgment. I've won from the people of Gadra their life-sustaining fish from Yamdro lake in an archery match. I thought taking the fish they wagered would save the lives of the fish in the lake. However, about a month after denying access to the fish, they are starving. Kindly revert with your fair judgment on whose lives I should save, the fish's or Gadrawas'.'

No sooner was the letter sent than the reply came from Lord of Death. 'Sentient beings are trapped in the web of karma, and I'm not in a position to save them all. It is not that my retinue and I are not compassionate, but we are fair in our judgment. No one can remove negative karma from beings until it is exhausted. The fish in Yamdro lake will be born as fish elsewhere if not in that lake. Without fish, Gadrawa will rob, kill and harm other animals. So, let the fish swim freely for them. But tell them to kill them quickly by cutting the nerve behind the gills and not torture them by throwing them on the hot sand.'

Drukpa Kunley promptly wrote to Lady Mermaid to release fish into Yamdro lake. The lake was once again thick with fish for Gadrawa.

Life returned to Nyapa Tshering's family; and to Gadra.

CHAPTER 18

When Karmapa was Smitten by Beauty

The quiet valley of north Yangpachen in Tibet, fringed with snow-covered mountains, spread far and wide. The grey valley was dotted with white sheep and black yaks. The flocks of sheep often seemed to merge with the small milky streams that flowed across the valley. The valley was so vast that everything appeared tiny, and every sound was faint.

One corner of the valley had turned into a garden of multiple hues. From a distance, the crowd looked like a colourful carpet sewn onto the valley floor. At a closer look, it was a heaving mass of people dressed and bejewelled in their best. Everybody—monks, nuns, men, women, children—sat on the ground quietly.

An empowerment ceremony[64] was underway.

An exquisitely beautiful girl called Ache Palzang stood out from the heaving crowd. Fair, elegant and beautifully dressed, a hint of blush lingered on her radiant face, as did a hint of a smile. She looked modest yet self-assured. She kept to herself, yet everybody in the crowd, including the presiding lama, had noticed her.

Suddenly, the quiet crowd was ripped apart by a loud cry which declared, 'Karmapa has lost his mental vow.' It came from a roughly dressed, ruggedly handsome man carrying a staff. 'Karmapa has lost his mental vow,' he shouted again, moving around the crowd, smiling broadly.

It hit the crowd like a stone hitting a flock of birds. The crowd was now abuzz with Karmapa's monks scurrying around to get to the man. 'Stop this blasphemy now, you mad scoundrel!' the monks cursed the man as they charged at him with sticks.

---

64 In Tibetan Buddhism, an empowerment ceremony—called *wang*—is a sacred ritual where a qualified teacher or lama grants permission and transmits the blessing to practise specific meditation techniques, usually related to a particular deity or tantric practice.

'Stop this. Don't beat him,' the Seventh Karmapa Chodrak Gyatsho said from his high throne. The highly revered lama sat on a throne decorated with colourful silk brocade. He wore maroon and orange silk robes, inner shirts with yellow linings, and a black hat scantily decorated with the golden images of crossed vajras, the sun and the moon. Over his head was a large parasol. In addition to being a distinguished scholar who had authored many important texts, Karmapa Chodrak Gyatsho actively engaged in impactful secular endeavours, such as mediating disputes, advocating for animal welfare and building bridges.

'Stop,' he repeated emphatically. 'He is a clairvoyant and can read others' minds. He is truly the reincarnation of the Indian adept Shavaripa.'

The crowd fell silent, and everybody turned to Karmapa. The charging monks froze. The shouting man stood calm and unperturbed.

'Just as human beings are drawn to animals with beautiful hair or feathers, a fleeting feeling of admiration crossed my mind on seeing this beautiful girl, although it did not amount to the feeling of attachment,' Karmapa confessed, 'and he read that feeling in me.'

'You're right, Drukpa Kunley,' Karmapa continued, turning to the disruptor. 'You're right. Now sing us a song about this beautiful girl.'

Drukpa Kunley instantly broke into a song.

> This fair-faced, demonic maiden
> She carries no hook or noose
> Yet with a mere sidelong glance
> She can conquer any discerning mind.
> I've seen her conquer a buddha's mind.

The loving, pleasing, soft whispers of
This charming, sweet-talking maiden
Pleasurable now, ends in heartbreak.

Her white skin augmented by a tinge of red
Her demeanour adorned by a smooth tongue
They helplessly pull you down to samsara
Desire not, seek not, Gyalwa Karmapa.

Then he said, 'The Himalayan monal pheasant eats aconite when it is hungry. It will kill them if other birds eat the same herb. I, Drukpa Kunley of Ralung, think of attractive girls like I do of mothers. It is dangerous for you, the high saint, to follow suit.'

'Who says you have the licence to do what others can't?' asked the monks.

'A letter from Vajradhara passed down through Tilopa and Naropa contains the licence and restrictions I've just spelt out,' Drukpa Kunley replied.

Karmapa was pleased with the response and smiled pleasantly. 'I'm more refined in conduct and discipline,' he remarked, 'but you are higher in terms of realization. You stand to be more popular in the future.'

As the crowd thinned and disappeared, Drukpa Kunley ambled away towards Sacha.

CHAPTER 19
Jamtrul's Donkey Incarnate

It was a big day at Jampa Lhakhang in Sacha. The monks were in a solemn mood. It was the death anniversary of their lama, Jamtrul Rinpoche, and they were saying prayers in the lama's memory.

Deep, soulful chanting reverberated across the temple halls warmed by hundreds of butter lamps flickering on the altar. Eyes half closed and palms joined, the monks looked truly meditative and prayerful.

Outside, a donkey was tethered to a post. It was overworked and its back was a bed of abscesses. It was underfed and seemed to brood over something. Its large ears were limp and drooping. Beneath its ashen snout lay a bunch of dry grass. As flies swarmed on its sore back, it swished its short tail across its thighs and flanks. It shook its head lazily and flailed its ears.

As some monks scurried around carrying pots and pans, an easy-going man stopped by the donkey and pulled it by the ear, saying to the monks, 'Give me your donkey for a while.'

The monks immediately recognized the man as Drukpa Kunley and protested, 'What's that, Drukpa Kunley?'

'It's a donkey,' Drukpa Kunley rejoined. 'What's making you busy today?'

'It's our lama's death anniversary, and we are praying for him,' said the monks.

'What was your lama called?'

'Jamtrul Rinpoche.'

'Jamtrul Rinpoche—where is he now?'

'He is in the heaven of Gaden.'

'Where is so-called Gaden?'

'Now you are asking too many questions, Drukpa,' the monks rebuked Drukpa Kunley sharply. 'Keep quiet and let us pray for our lama.'

The monks joined their palms in supplication, closed their eyes, and prayed:

The embodiment of dharmakaya and five wisdoms, the eternal fount of blessings; homage to the Emanated One. Shower your blessings on us.

Drukpa Kunley turned to the donkey and prayed:

The wretched life of a donkey; unfed and burdened with three measures of load. Homage to one whose hips are whipped and flogged.

'Now, why are you praying to the donkey?' The monks yelled at Drukpa Kunley. 'You know it's our lama's death anniversary, not your donkey's.'

'This donkey is your lama,' Drukpa Kunley told them. The donkey stared at him, eyes glistening with tears. It was as though the donkey had recognized Drukpa Kunley and understood what he had just said.

'This can't be,' the monks protested. 'Why would our lama be born as a donkey?'

'Your lama had travelled across India, Tibet and Mongolia burdening horses and donkeys with extremely heavy loads,' said Drukpa Kunley. 'He's paying for that now.'

As he stroked the drooping ears, the donkey shed a torrent of tears. The argumentative monks were now ashen-faced and speechless. They looked at one another, lost for words. Before them stood their lama, a revered man, trapped in the body of a weeping animal.

After a long, uneasy moment, a senior monk turned to Drukpa Kunley and asked when their lama would be reborn as a human. Drukpa Kunley told the monks to feed the donkey well for five years and, after its death, wait for good news from Lithang in Kham.

'Let's see how accurate his prediction is,' said the monks, and fed the donkey well.

Five years later, the sulky animal collapsed and died.

A few years later, the monks heard that Jamtrul Rinpoche's reincarnation was born in Lithang.

CHAPTER 20

Sacha's Girl and the Dawn Within

As dawn broke over the towering Himalaya, euphoria pervaded Lhacho Drolma's whole being. She sat cross-legged on a thin mat. It had been three years since the first time she had sat on the same mat with a sense of intimidation and uncertainty. Today, her mind became as clear and luminous as the autumn sky without a speck of a cloud. She felt a dawn breaking within her, far more radiant and luminous than the one breaking over the Himalaya. Infinite knowledge dawned on her. Her body felt light and buoyant as if it had been released from the shackles of all things material. All discriminatory concepts and thoughts suddenly left her. She felt free. She felt liberated. She *was* liberated.

Lhacho Drolma was among the thirteen girls from the entire cis-Himalayan region closest to Drukpa Kunley's heart. She attained liberation after meditating in the mountains of Jomolhari. Three years earlier, she was not known as Lhacho Drolma. She was a lay girl named Loleg Buthri.

Drukpa Kunley was in Sacha when he came across Loleg Buthri, an irresistibly beautiful maiden he desired. But she rejected his sexual advances. He felt embarrassed and insulted. 'This is a conceited girl,' he said to himself. Other girls considered sexual intercourse with him a rare opportunity for spiritual awakening.

He had barely walked a hundred metres from Loleg Buthri's house when he found himself repeating, 'This is a conceited girl.' In another fit of embarrassment, he stomped his foot on a flat rock. The heel of his foot sank into the rock and left a distinct impression.

The news about the incident rapidly spread across Sacha. Hundreds of people flocked to the rock to see Drukpa Kunley's footprint. It was the talk of the village. But the biggest topic of conversation was how Loleg Buthri had denied herself an opportunity most girls would die for.

With more and more people talking about it, the magnitude of the opportunity she had missed dawned on Loleg Buthri. She repented in silence, and her repentance grew by the day until it was too overpowering for her. She went to meet Drukpa Kunley.

'I failed to recognize you as a buddha,' she said. 'Please forgive me and give me another opportunity.'

Drukpa Kunley sat back and sipped the chang Loleg Buthri had brought him. He did not show any emotion. He seemed to pay more attention to the chang than Loleg Buthri.

'Show me your vagina,' he said after a long while like a businessman doing a hard-nosed transaction. As she lifted her wrap-around and bared her vagina, he pulled down his angdar and pulled out his penis. He took a quick look at both the organs and declared, 'Alas, our things won't dovetail. Mine needs a round hole, but yours is triangular.'

Loleg Buthri turned red and did not know how to react. Then she quickly composed herself and made the next request. 'Ideally,' she said, 'please take me with you. If you won't do this, send me to a solitary hermitage. If you won't do this either, please cut my hair and give me a spiritual name.'

'I can't do the first one,' Drukpa Kunley said. 'I'm a wandering yogi without the means to even fend for myself. And you can't do the second. The third proposition looks doable. What kind of name do you want?'

Loleg Buthri could not think of a particular kind of name. She wrung her hands and looked around as if to find a clue. She looked at Drukpa Kunley for a cue, but he did not even blink. 'Something all-encompassing,' she finally blurted out.

'Take Sachu Melung Namkha Drolma[65],' Drukpa Kunley said.

---

65 ས་ཆུ་མེ་རླུང་ནམ་མཁའ་སྒྲོལ་མ་ (Earth Water Fire Air Sky Drolma)

|| SACHA'S GIRL AND THE DAWN WITHIN || 111

'Not this, please. Something more pleasing,' requested Loleg Buthri.

'Then take Piwang Lingbu Dranyen Drolma[66].'

'This one is a little discomfiting,' she said, 'maybe something fearsome.'

'Then it should be Tagzik Domdrey Dugdrul Drolma[67].'

'These are the names of animals,' she said. 'Give me something that sounds softer and smoother.'

'Then take Dardang Goechen Mentsi Drolma[68],' Drukpa Kunley said with a smile.

Loleg Buthri was now growing impatient. 'Naljorpa, you are now being mischievous with me,' she said. 'Can you give me an appealing name?'

'Here it is,' Drukpa Kunley said. 'Kara Buram Drangtsi Drolma[69].'

'None of these please me,' she said. 'Please give me a name that describes my intention to renounce the mundane world, practise the dharma, and take refuge in a lama.'

'Zhenlog Choje Sachab Drolma[70],' he said. 'Are you happy with this?'

'No. Not really,' she said.

'Then take Jodod Ngotsha Lhacho[71] Drolma,' Drukpa Kunley said.

---

66 པི་ཝང་གླིང་བུ་སྒྲ་སྙན་སྒྲོལ་མ། (Fiddle Flute Lute Drolma)

67 སྟག་གཟིག་དོམ་དྲེད་དུག་སྦྲུལ་སྒྲོལ་མ། (Tiger Leopard Bear Snake Drolma)

68 དར་དང་གོས་ཆེན་སྨན་རྩི་སྒྲོལ་མ། (Silk Brocade Scarf Drolma)

69 ཀ་ར་བུ་རམ་སྦྲང་རྩི་སྒྲོལ་མ། (Sugar Malasses Honey Drolma)

70 ཞེན་ལོག་ཆོས་བྱས་སྐྱབས་སྒྲོལ་མ། (Renunciating Practising Refuge-seeking Drolma)

71 ཇོ་འདོད་ངོ་ཚ་ལྷ་ཆོས་སྒྲོལ་མ། (Lustful but Ashamed Dharma Drolma)

'Can I drop the first part and take Lhacho Drolma?' she asked.
'All right,' he said. 'You are now Lhacho Drolma.'

In the naming process, Drukpa Kunley learnt about her potential for spiritual awakening and decided to grant her second request. He sent her to a secluded hermitage in the mountains of Jomolhari.

That was the first time Lhacho Drolma felt the dawn of a new life breaking within her.

CHAPTER 21

The Burden of Breaking a Bow and Ploughshare

As Drukpa Kunley wandered aimlessly across the vast expanse of the Tibetan landscape, he crossed paths with people from all walks of life. He drank chang, chit-chatted and sang folk songs with humble servants in taverns and village dwellings. He drank tea, debated and sang philosophical songs with decorated monastic leaders full of self-importance. He ate and drank and rubbed shoulders with powerful lords who lived an opulent life without a trace of humility. He also met indolent beggars who would sit and languish rather than work and earn.

He effortlessly blended perfectly with all of them, displaying a remarkable ability to connect with people, regardless of their station in life. He was an unconventional spiritual practitioner who was deeply rooted in reality. At times, he was uncouth and boorish; at other times, he was elegant and sophisticated. To servants, he appeared as a kindred spirit who was content with the simple pleasures of life. Monks saw him as an erudite scholar with a rebellious streak. Lords thought he was a wandering eccentric, seeking only chang and women. Beggars thought he was no different from them, except for his melodious voice and adventurous spirit. Drukpa Kunley embodied all these personas and yet transcended them. He belonged to none exclusively.

The servants he encountered were deliriously happy with a few cups of chang after their masters sent them home in the evening. The monks he encountered turned their spiritual pursuit into a regimental lifestyle rather than training the mind. The rich people he encountered turned all their wealth and luxury into misery by grumbling and moaning endlessly.

Once, Drukpa Kunley was roaming the countryside with his dog when he came across a servant. He relished traversing Tibet's rugged countryside where both nature and people had largely retained the innocence and sanity of a contented life.

The servant said to Drukpa Kunley, 'How wonderful it would be if I were a lord.' He expressed envy towards lords, longing for their perceived power and privilege.

'You are naive and you say so because you haven't been one,' Drukpa Kunley remarked with a knowing smile. 'There is no life more miserable than a lord's.'

'How is that possible when a lord can command everything at will?' asked the servant, puzzled. A minor lord who stood beside the servant was equally puzzled. 'How could a lord's life be more miserable than a servant's?' he wondered. 'How could servitude be better than lordship?' They looked at Drukpa Kunley curiously, expecting an explanation.

Drukpa Kunley looked at them like a teacher looks at his confused students and explained, 'Here's how a servant's life can be better than a lord's. If a lord has the merit to command respect, his life becomes bearable. Otherwise, no life can be more miserable than his.

'If he is too strong, he will break the bow. If he is too weak, he can't launch an arrow. If his law is too stringent, everybody will resent it. If his law is too lenient, he can't even order a bag of flour.

'He must be prepared to break his own ploughshare tilling common land. If he is compassionate, people will become spoiled. If he rebukes them, people will take offence. If he gives them land, they will not pay taxes. If he does not, they will go to the extent of offering their uncle's barn to appeal for it. Even lords have to pay taxes. Therefore, it is happier to be an average servant than a lord.'

'You are right,' the servant said. 'I never realized that being a lord can be so hard. I'm happy being a servant now.'

The minor lord could identify with all the burdens of being a lord Drukpa Kunley had elucidated. 'You are absolutely right,' he acknowledged. 'How I wish I were a servant!'

Drukpa Kunley smiled and chuckled softly. 'You are absolutely wrong,' he said. 'You have no idea how miserable a servant's life can be. You are naive because you haven't been one.'

The minor lord was utterly baffled. 'But you just said that it was better to be a servant than a lord.'

'No, I didn't,' Drukpa Kunley said, 'I said it was better to be a servant if someone did not have what it took to be a lord.'

'Ah, I get it,' said the minor lord.

'Do not wish to be a servant, my friend,' Drukpa Kunley continued. 'It's better to be a lord than a servant, however burdensome. To be a servant is hard. If you are a capable servant, you won't even have time to eat. The whole of your body, speech and mind would be fully engaged in a way that you wouldn't find respite. If you are not capable, everybody will drive you away. Even villagers will treat you with contempt.

If you are physically strong, you will be deployed to bring down stronger lords and their fortresses. If you are not physically strong, even your wife will beat you up. If you have wealth, you will attract everyone's attention. All kinds of people, including thieves, will look at you with an avaricious eye. If you do not have wealth, people will call you a hungry beggar and humiliate you in public.'

'This is so true,' the servant acknowledged, adding that he could identify with the plight of a servant.

'You are absolutely right, Naljorpa,' observed the minor lord. 'Now, I don't want to be a servant. I'm a small lord. Yet, a small lord is far better than an illustrious servant.'

'It's not easy being either if you lack the merit and tact to be one,' concluded Drukpa Kunley.

'Certainly true. Indeed true,' said the servant and the minor lord in unison.

CHAPTER 22

Subduing Fearsome Spears and Dogs

A Kongpo man was furious and fuming. He pressed a spear against Drukpa Kunley's chest. 'Why should I give you my spears that I've risked my life for?' he demanded.

Drukpa Kunley was in Lhasa surrounded by a group of men from Kongpo in south-eastern Tibet carrying loads of spears. He asked them to give him a spear, which enraged the heavily burdened men. Spears were expensive, and trading them demanded heavy investments and extreme physical hardships. Therefore, a random mendicant with a brass neck casually asking for a spear was provocative and insulting.

'Either you are stupid or trying to trivialize our trade,' said the man. The spear was pointed at his chest but Drukpa Kunley was not intimidated. He did not even look at the man. He looked at the ornate spear and smiled expansively. The shaft of the spear was slender, sharp and shiny. Its wooden handle was decorated with a skull motif. The men were surprised by Drukpa Kunley's casual dismissal of the lethal weapon.

As the traders curiously observed Drukpa Kunley, he snatched the spear and said, 'Let's see which one is stronger—your spear of ignorance or my spear of primordial awareness.' He pulled the spear from the two ends and stretched it like an elastic band. He then twisted it into a knot.

The Kongpo men were astounded. They looked at the twisted spear, agape. 'Are you not human?' asked the man who pointed the spear at him. 'Are you a ghost or a malevolent spirit? If not, you must be a great yogi. Who are you?'

'I can be whoever you believe I am,' said Drukpa Kunley. 'It doesn't make any difference to me.'

Another man stepped forward and offered his backload of spears to Drukpa Kunley. 'Please forgive us for asking if you are a ghost or a malevolent spirit,' he apologized. Drukpa Kunley was neither aggrieved by the act of aggression nor buoyed by the apology. He simply gave the knotted spear to this man and walked away.

Sometime later, a chieftain of Kham gave the man twenty-one villages in exchange for the knotted spear.

By this time, Drukpa Kunley was in Rinpung, southwest of Lhasa. He was standing in front of the Rinpung chieftain's castle, wearing gold, silver and other precious jewels. He had a white silk scarf tied around his body. 'I'm bejewelled and burdened today,' he said. 'How do I look?'

Before him stood a crowd of courtiers and behind him, the chieftain of Rinpung, who had offered Drukpa Kunley jewels from his treasury. All of them were awestruck by a miracle Drukpa Kunley had performed.

The chieftain had invited Drukpa Kunley to his castle to verify the rumours of his miraculous powers. A courtier told Drukpa Kunley to wait at the gate as he walked ahead to chain the two massive watchdogs. But Drukpa Kunley did not heed him and walked right behind him, swinging a willow twig.

Before the courtier could chain the dogs—one white and the other black—Drukpa Kunley was face to face with them. As the dogs pounced on him, he swiftly lashed the willow twig to cut them into two equal halves, saying, 'Why are the dogs completely white and completely black?'

For a brief, intense moment, the four mutilated parts rolled about violently before the white hindquarters joined the black forequarters and the black hindquarters joined the white forequarters. The two new creatures, half-white and half-black, jumped about gleefully as if nothing had happened to them.

'Truly unbelievable!' exclaimed the courtiers. 'Truly miraculous!'

The chieftain was so stunned by the new incarnations of his dogs that he kept gazing at them until Drukpa Kunley said, 'You will never finish wondering about Kunga Legpa's foolery and lunacy. Instead, you must devote your time to chanting mani, for death is uncertain.' He sang a sermon on mani.

The chieftain and all the courtiers were deeply moved by Drukpa Kunley's miraculous powers and sermon on mani. They prostrated before him and committed themselves to chanting mani. Then, the chieftain handed over the keys to his treasury to Drukpa Kunley, offering whatever and however much he desired.

Drukpa Kunley took the keys and joked that he would empty the treasury. He wore a few pieces of jewellery, stepped out in front of the castle, and said, 'I'm bejewelled and burdened today. How do I look?'

Before the crowd could have a good look at the rarely adorned Drukpa Kunley, he returned all the jewellery to the chieftain. The chieftain insisted that he take them, but Drukpa Kunley declined, saying, 'I've worn them once. Nobody will wear them forever.'

CHAPTER 23

Breaking Ngawang Chogyal's Shackles of Avarice

Early one morning, Drukpa Kunley found himself among a throng of monks from Ralung by the banks of the Tsangpo river in Tibet, awaiting boats for crossing. Incognito and without a destination in mind, he stood there observing the bustling scene where groups of people jostled for passage.

The first rays of the sun shimmered on the mighty river, whose course was believed to have been carved by a bodhisattva to bring life-giving water to the parched land. The Tsangpo's course was dotted with sacred monasteries and sites drawing people from across the vast country. However, crossing the river on crudely made yak hide boats was an everyday challenge for most Tibetans. Frequent squabbles and fights broke out on its banks.

The riverbank was a cacophony of noises as brash boatmen noisily pushed and shoved people rushing to their boats. The monks of Ralung rushed to one of the three boats but the loud boatman pushed them away from his boat. Drukpa Kunley stood behind them, aloof and unhurried. Stepping back in exasperation, the monks asked Drukpa Kunley, 'Where are you from and where are you headed? You don't seem eager to catch a boat.'

Now that the monks of Ralung had spoken to him, he instantly cooked up a travel plan. 'I'm going to Ralung to meet Lama Ngawang Chogyal and beg for something he is willing to grant me.'

The monks looked at Drukpa Kunley from head to toe, finding him strangely dressed and carrying a bow and a quiver. They thought he was a smooth-talking beggar with rugged good looks. He looked mysteriously self-assured and confident for a beggar. Beside him sat his dog.

'You may not realize how busy Ön Rinpoche is, managing both spiritual and temporal affairs at Ralung,' one of them remarked. 'You cannot meet him at all if he is in retreat.'

BREAKING NGAWANG CHOGYAL'S SHACKLES OF AVARICE

Another cacophony of voices erupted on the bank as another boat arrived and the waiting people rushed to it. The monks of Ralung did not seem eager to try their luck this time. 'More boats will come,' one of them assured the others. The same monk turned to Drukpa Kunley and said, 'Even if you can meet him, it's doubtful you will get anything from him because he has grown more avaricious in recent days.'

Drukpa Kunley smiled and said, 'Your lama shouldn't be as tight-fisted as you describe him. I'm going to meet him anyway. There is another reason for me to go to Ralung. I've heard that Nyonpa Drukpa Kunley is going to stage a public show called "Breaking Ngawang Chogyal's Shackles of Avarice". It promises to be highly entertaining. You shouldn't miss it.'

Amused, the monks chuckled among themselves. 'Breaking Ön Rinpoche's shackles of avarice? Is that even possible?' one quipped.

The leader of the group, a stern-looking senior monk, said, 'Our Rinpoche's shackles are as unbreakable as iron chains. I doubt whether this wanderer who has abandoned his spiritual lineage can ever break them. But if he dares to attempt it publicly, we will be there to witness the show.'

Other monks joined him, 'If it's truly entertaining, why not? You can go ahead. We will join you after our work here is done.'

When a boat returned to the bank, the monks of Ralung clambered aboard, leaving no room for Drukpa Kunley and his dog. As all the passengers had already crossed over to the other side, and no boat was forthcoming, Drukpa Kunley found himself stranded with his dog.

However, on the opposite bank, an empty boat lay waiting. Calling out to the boatman, Drukpa Kunley requested passage across the river for himself and his dog. 'I can't come back for just you and your dog unless you pay me a hefty fare,' the boatman demanded.

'All right,' said Drukpa Kunley. 'Then, tell your boat not to follow me.' With a subtle gesture, he beckoned the empty boat, which swiftly glided across the river to his side, much to the astonishment of the boatman. The boatman frantically ran up and down the bank shouting, 'Release my boat please!'

Then he hurried across an iron bridge hundreds of metres downstream and came over to Drukpa Kunley. Offering him chang, he begged for forgiveness for being rude.

Drukpa Kunley reached Ralung by midday and presented himself before Lama Ngawang Chogyal. Curious, Lama Ngawang Chogyal enquired about his sudden arrival. Drukpa Kunley said he was coming from Mon, where humble nomads had requested him to bestow empowerment on them. They thought they could not afford to invite Lama Ngawang Chogyal. When he said he did not have the customary instruments and attire for the ritual, they assured him that Ön Rinpoche would be generous to lend all the necessary ritual accoutrements.

Lama Ngawang Chogyal felt obliged to lend his instruments and attire. 'You can take them all as long as you take good care of them,' he said, handing him a brocade cloak, a meditation hat and a set of religious instruments.

The following day, Drukpa Kunley made a public announcement regarding an empowerment ceremony aimed at breaking the shackles of avarice. He invited all the monks and lay people to gather in the meadow at the base of a barren hill overlooking Ralung Monastery. He particularly wanted those who thought Lama Ngawang Chogyal was avaricious to attend the ceremony.

BREAKING NGAWANG CHOGYAL'S SHACKLES OF AVARICE

A huge crowd gathered to partake in Drukpa Kunley's empowerment ceremony, prompting Lama Ngawang Chogyal to worry about what the mad Drukpa might do. So, he dispatched two of his attendants to observe the proceedings.

As the audience settled, Drukpa Kunley climbed the summit of the hill clad in the brocade garments Lama Ngawang Chogyal had lent him. Strapping his belongings to his body, he brandished a drum, bell and vajra before rolling down the steep incline proclaiming, 'This is how Drukpa Kunley breaks the shackles of Choje Ngawang Chogyal's avarice.'

The spectacle of Drukpa Kunley tumbling down the hill like a huge ball of brocade, accompanied by a cloud of dust and the resounding beats of drum and bell left the onlookers stunned. Upon his landing in the meadow, many feared the worst, assuming he had succumbed to the violent fall. Shocked, they momentarily forgot about Lama Ngawang Chogyal's invaluable empowerment items and robes. Lama Ngawang Chogyal could not look at his precious items and robes being destroyed. He stood devastated momentarily before realizing it was his avarice that had made them precious.

However, to their amazement, Drukpa Kunley emerged completely unscathed, with every article of clothing and religious instrument intact, without even a speck of dust on them. However, having confronted his meaningless attachment to religious items and robes, Lama Ngawang Chogyal did not feel a sense of relief.

CHAPTER 24

A Herd of Meat for Tsang Desi

It was late afternoon in Rawa in the Tsang province of Central Tibet. The haughty and autocratic governor of Tsang, Deb Morong, emerged from his imposing palace accompanied by a retinue of courtiers who tiptoed by his sides. He wore a colourful, flowing brocade gown and a large fur hat. He walked slowly and paused frequently to turn right and left to talk to his courtiers. Every few steps, he passed an order to a courtier, with stony gravity.

Just as the governor was starting to enjoy talking to his men in the quiet surroundings, a melodic voice accompanied by gentle strains of a Tibetan lute wafted through the air. The song was harshly punctuated by a cacophony of excited noise. At a distance, they saw a man wildly hugging, kissing and fondling a local girl named Adzoma.

The governor looked disapprovingly at the unruly public display of affection and asked, 'Who could that fellow be?'

A courtier promptly replied, 'The man from Ralung called Drukpa Kunley.'

'Ah, the one who wanders around the country in the guise of a religious man committing all manner of atrocity,' the governor said angrily. 'The people of Ralung didn't pay their meat tax last year. Tell him to come here forthwith.'

Drukpa Kunley was swiftly brought before the governor.

'I gather you are the madman Drukpa Kunley,' the governor growled. 'Do you remember that the people of Ralung had to pay one yak and nine sheep in taxes to Yamdro Nangkartse in addition to wool and meat to Tsechen? Instead of being grateful to me for exempting all those taxes, you have killed and eaten all my blue sheep around the hermitage in Gaden and harmed the people of Gaden in numerous ways. Now prepare to pay me one hundred animal carcasses in taxes tomorrow.'

Drukpa Kunley listened to the tirade with an air of elegant nonchalance. When the governor paused, he said, 'Whatever needs to be paid shall be paid according to the records of our deeds kept by the Lord of Death. But if you insist on meat, it shall be paid, too. Leave your gates open tomorrow morning.'

As Drukpa Kunley walked away, the officials wondered aloud how he might bring one hundred carcasses. Some of them concluded that he will surely rustle cattle. 'If meat is delivered to me, I don't care how he brings it,' the governor said sternly, putting the officials' murmuring to rest.

As the first rays of the sun hit the hills of Rawa the following morning, the rumble of a stampeding herd could be heard from the Gyangtse valley. Within moments, a herd of one hundred blue sheep of Gaden came crashing and clomping through the open gates of the governor's palace. Closely following the herd was Drukpa Kunley.

'Pen them up now if you want the meat tax, or you won't see them again,' he told the governor, who stood back, astonished. 'Take all of them, or I have the permission of the Lord of Death to send them to heaven.'

'You mad Drukpa, you are either the devil incarnate or an emanation of a buddha,' stammered the governor. 'It's astounding how you drive these wild animals like docile sheep! But I'll take only meat, not live animals.'

'Then meat you shall have,' declared Drukpa Kunley and started beheading and skinning the animals. As the frightened governor receded even further, a mountain of bloody carcasses piled up before him—a jumble of heads, bodies and skins. 'Here's your meat now,' he told the governor.

The governor now stood stripped of his kingly pride that lent him a deep voice and a snobbish tone. 'What a terrible thing we have done!' he stammered. 'I don't want the meat. Take it and sell it in the market and liberate the souls of these poor animals.'

'You demanded meat, so I brought you meat,' Drukpa Kunley said. 'If you don't want their meat, the animals can go back to the hills of Gaden.'

As he snapped his fingers and told the animals to go back home, all the carcasses rose from the heap, frantically wearing their own skins and picking up random heads. The animals rushed back to Gaden, big ones carrying small odd heads and small ones carrying big odd heads.

As the stampeding herd disappeared and calm returned to the palace like a hush after a storm, the mighty governor and his courtiers, reduced to tears, bowed down before Drukpa Kunley. They had discovered the madman of Ralung; and themselves.

CHAPTER 25

Prostrating to Palkhor Stupa and the Gyangtse Girl

PROSTRATING TO PALKHOR STUPA | 131

'You killed and resurrected all those animals yesterday. It was a moving spectacle that inspired great devotion in us. You must certainly have been a buddha in a past life,' said young maidens surrounding Drukpa Kunley in the bustling tavern of Adzoma.

Drukpa Kunley was in the same tavern two days ago, drinking and singing, when the governor of Tsang, Deb Morong, had summoned him and demanded one hundred animal carcasses as taxes.

Drukpa Kunley chuckled softly, taking a sip from his cup. He was half-drunk. 'My past lives are not abundantly clear to me, but my habits offer a clue.'

'Please, tell us about it then,' the maidens pleaded eagerly.

'I'll give it a try,' said Drukpa Kunley and began.
In the cycle of countless lives,
There's no life I haven't lived.
It's not crystal clear to me;
It appears something like this.
Since I'm obsessed with chang,
I may have been a bee.
Since I'm carnal and lustful,
I may have been a rooster.
Since I'm angry and resentful,
I may have been a serpent.
Since I'm indolent and ignorant,
I may have been a pig.
Since I'm greedy and covetous,
I may have been a rich person.
Since I'm bald-faced and shameless,
I may have been a mad person.

> Since I'm a habitual liar,
> I may have been a charlatan.
> Since I'm rude and boorish,
> I may have been a monkey.
> Since I'm savage and cold,
> I may have been a wolf.
> Since I have a tight anus,
> I may have been a nun.
> Since I'm meticulous,
> I may have been childless.
> Since I survive on offerings,
> I may have been a lama.
> Since I'm avaricious and thrifty,
> I may have been a lama's attendant.
> Since I'm self-centred and vain,
> I may have been a mighty lord.
> Since I'm dishonest and deceitful,
> I may have been a businessman.
> Since I'm glib and garrulous,
> I may have been a woman.

'I'm not sure if it rings true. What do you think about it?' asked Drukpa Kunley.

'On the pretext of telling us about your past lives, you have exposed all our flaws,' observed the girls. 'But thank you all the same.'

From Adzoma's tavern, Drukpa Kunley drifted to Palkhor Stupa in Gyangtse in the Tsang province. Palkhor Stupa was built in 1427 by a Gyangtse prince. The nine-storey stupa was the largest in Tibet, housing one hundred and eight chapels. The stupa housed a monastic school where monks were engaged in a vigorous metaphysical debate when Drukpa Kunley arrived.

Two monks were taking on each other, surrounded by their classmates. It was a noisy affair. One of them was seated; the other stood before him, stomping his left foot and violently hitting the palm of the outstretched left hand with that of the right. He was the challenger. He punctuated every question by smacking his right palm on the left with explosive force. His opponent, the defender, was less mobile and hence, physically less aggressive, but shouted back his replies with equal gusto.

Drukpa Kunley observed the drama with little interest because his attention was diverted by a beautiful girl standing by the corner of the stupa. The girl stood quietly, pulling on a rosary. Her long, black hair was braided. Her slender figure was sharply silhouetted against the stupa's glistening white wall. For him, the calmly dignified figure of the Gyangtse girl was more arresting than the noisy spectacle put up by the monks.

All the while, an elderly monk was observing Drukpa Kunley with indifference. As Drukpa Kunley trivialized the noisy debate with a sly smile, the monk challenged him, 'Drukpa Kunley, it is fascinating that you can perform all kinds of miracles with natural ease and spontaneity. Yet, your behaviour is directly against the Buddha's teachings because you refuse to prostrate to the stupa and the assembly of monks.'

Drukpa Kunley did not feel surprised or challenged by the question. He smiled and said, 'Prostration is for you all, not me. I'm a yogi who transcended prostration and atoning for sins a long time ago. If you insist, I can do it.'

He prostrated to the stupa, chanting this:

> I prostrate to this beautiful mound of earth
> Not counted among the eight Sugata stupas[72].
> I prostrate to this splendid piece of architecture
> Not created by the hands of Vishvakarman[73].
> I prostrate to the Thirteen Wheels[74]
> Far removed from the thirteenth bhumi[75].
> I prostrate to the bottom of the Gyangtse girl
> Not analogous to the body of Goddess Tara.

'Alas! This is disgusting!' exclaimed the monks. 'Drukpa Kunley is truly a madman. This is utterly insane.'

'A woman is worth prostrating to like a stupa,' Drukpa Kunley said. 'Here's why. She is generally the fount of all things good and bad. Therefore, she is the mother of all wisdom. Besides, the sum of all the moral vows religious practitioners receive from their masters in exchange for precious gold and silver is enshrined as a mandala between her legs.'

The lay people watching the exchange burst out laughing. The monks took offence and looked scornfully at Drukpa Kunley.

---

[72] The eight Sugata stupas represent eight important events in the life of Lord Buddha. They are the Stupa of Lotus Petals, the Stupa of Enlightenment, the Stupa with Many Auspicious Doors, the Stupa of Miracles, the Stupa of Lord Buddha's Descent from the Trayastrimsa Heaven, the Stupa of Reconciliation, the Stupa of Complete Victory, and the Stupa of Parinirvana.

[73] The craftsman of gods worshipped as the god of crafts and artisans.

[74] The thirteen wheels refers to the discs that make the tower of the stupa.

[75] Bhumis in Mahayana Buddhism represent the stages a practitioner reaches on the path to enlightenment.

The discipline master accosted him with a stick and said, 'We are observing the purest form of moral vow here. Why do you make fun of us?'

Drukpa Kunley exited the scene calmly, singing a song that condemned the extravagant trappings of monastic order and ranks, which may divert them from the true path to enlightenment. 'I cannot match the scholarly stature of the monks of Palkhor Stupa,' he concluded. 'Yet, Ralung's Drukpa Kunley is not an uninitiated novice. Let's wait and see who truly finds the light of enlightenment.'

CHAPTER 26

Entrusting Old Shoes to Jowo Shakyamuni

ENTRUSTING OLD SHOES TO JOWO SHAKYAMUNI

While spending some time with Palzang Buthri in Lhasa, Drukpa Kunley decided to visit the Jokhang temple, not out of religious piety, but to observe what the devotees visiting and circumambulating the temple were actually doing.

The ancient temple, initially built in the seventh century as Rasa Thrulnang by the Nepali queen of King Songtsen Gampo, Princess Bhrikuti, housed the revered Jowo Shakyamuni, a statue of Lord Buddha at the age of twelve. The statue, crafted from the most precious materials on earth, was believed to date back to Lord Buddha himself. It was brought to Tibet by Princess Wencheng, the Chinese queen of King Songtsen Gampo.

Drukpa Kunley strode casually into the temple where the serene statue of Jowo Shakyamuni sat upon a resplendent and jewel-studded throne. Seated in the lotus position, its golden visage shimmered in the soft reddish glow cast by flickering butter lamps. Rather than offering prostrations, Drukpa Kunley removed his worn-out leather shoes and hung them from the ears of the statue, entrusting them with this request, 'Please look after them until I complete my circumambulation around you and return to collect them.'

As he made his way out, Drukpa Kunley saw dozens of people engaged in clockwise circumambulation around the temple. Each person held a rosary, murmuring prayers as they briskly moved along, their attention fixed on moving forward without exchanging words or glances. Drukpa Kunley stood out as the only person walking around the temple at a leisurely pace, unnoticed by the bustling crowd.

As he rounded a corner, he came upon a man sitting cross-legged with his back straight against the wall of the temple. With palms turned upwards, resting gently on his lap, and eyes closed in peaceful repose, the man appeared calm and relaxed. After observing him for several minutes, Drukpa Kunley approached him and asked, 'What are you so serious and meditative about, sitting all alone?'

The man opened his eyes but did not reply to Drukpa Kunley, who asked again, 'What are you so serious and meditative about, sitting all alone?'

'I'm practising patience, for it embodies the essence of the dharma,' replied the man, closing his eyes again.

'It's a very good practice,' Drukpa Kunley remarked before continuing his circumambulation.

After completing one round and returning to the man, Drukpa Kunley repeated the question, 'What are you so serious and meditative about, sitting all alone?' The man opened his eyes to find the same man asking the same question. Yet, he answered him the same way, 'I'm practising patience, for it embodies the essence of the dharma.'

Drukpa Kunley completed another round and came back to the man with the same question. Once again, the man opened his eyes to see the familiar figure standing before him, asking the same question. He gave the same answer but this time grudgingly.

In the meantime, the caretaker returned to the temple and was taken aback to find a pair of old shoes dangling from the ears of Jowo Shakyamuni. 'What a sacrilegious act, whosoever has committed it!' he exclaimed in horror, proceeding to remove the shoes. However, before his hand could reach them, Jowo Shakyamuni spoke, 'Do not touch them. Druk Nyon Kunga Legpa has entrusted them to me.' Startled, the caretaker recoiled and withdrew.

Drukpa Kunley completed yet another round and asked the sitting man the same question. The man, visibly irritated, opened his eyes and rolled them. 'What are you so serious and meditative about, sitting all alone?' Drukpa Kunley persisted. This time, the man refused to answer him. His face was no longer calm.

'It's a very good practice if you can do it sitting,' remarked Drukpa Kunley, strolling away. The man cast a dark glance after Drukpa Kunley.

Upon completing another round and returning to the man, Drukpa Kunley observed his face twitching with irritation. Yet, his eyes remained closed and his posture straight. 'What are you so serious and meditative about, sitting all alone?' asked Drukpa Kunley, smiling.

The man opened his eyes to find Drukpa Kunley once again standing before him. 'Would you let me practise patience in peace?' he barked, fuming with anger.

'Carry on with your patience,' said Drukpa Kunley calmly, walking away.

As he approached the man once again, he tiptoed towards him, hesitating to repeat the same question. Despite his closed eyes, his tense posture betrayed his inner turmoil.

Unable to contain his amusement, Drukpa Kunley let out a chuckle. Startled, the man opened his eyes and demanded, 'It's you again, what do you want?'

'I simply want to know what you are so serious and meditative about, sitting all alone,' said Drukpa Kunley, chuckling heartily.

Exploding with fury, the man sprang up and chased after him, yelling, 'These wandering beggars won't let me practise patience in peace. Now you'll see what I'm serious and meditative about.'

Drukpa Kunley dashed around the temple, shouting, 'The practitioner of patience is furious and wants to beat me up!' The crowd around the temple burst into laughter, causing the man to retreat in embarrassment.

After some time, Drukpa Kunley returned inside the temple to retrieve his shoes. As he put them on, the caretaker approached him respectfully, making a request, 'Druk Nyon, you are widely known for your wit, humour and profound insights. Can you compose a praise for Jowo Shakyamuni?'

Drukpa Kunley said he was not qualified to compose anything for Jowo. However, upon the caretaker's insistence, he proceeded to chant the following lines, offering prostrations before the statue.

> You and I stood as equals in days of yore;
> Diligence has turned you into a buddha,
> Indolence has chained me to samsara.
> Today, I humbly prostrate at your feet.[76]

The short prayer beautifully highlighted the presence of inherent buddha nature in all sentient beings, that latent bud obscured by afflictive emotions and indolence, ready to blossom into perfect buddhahood with the union of perseverance and dedication.

As he exited the temple, Drukpa Kunley reflected on the man he had encountered outside. With the seed of buddhahood ever present in him, he envisioned the man taking a significant stride towards enlightenment on the day his practice of patience bore fruit.

---

76 པོ་ཉི་ཁྱེད་དང་ངེད་མཉམ་པ་ལ། ཁྱེད་ཉི་བརྩོན་པ་འགྲུས་ཀྱིས་སངས་རྒྱས་ཤིང་། ངེད་ལ་ལེ་ལོས་འཁོར་བར་འཁྱམས། དེ་རིང་ཁྱེད་ཀྱི་ཞབས་ལ་ཕྱག་འཚལ།

CHAPTER 27

Monks Steal Drukpa Kunley's Afflictive Emotions

The marketplace of Lhasa pulsated with the vibrant energy of merchants, pilgrims, nomads, monks and musicians. Situated against the majestic backdrop of the Himalaya, it was a cultural melting pot drawing people from across the Himalayan region.

Stalls and vendors lined the narrow streets, their colourful wares—exotic spices, textiles, jewellery and precious metals—spilling onto the cobblestone pathways. Tibetan nomads in traditional attire haggled over goods and livestock alongside merchants clad in silk robes.

Amid the hustle, monks and pilgrims from distant lands mingled with traders and travellers, sharing stories and spreading news and gossip.

Suddenly, Drukpa Kunley burst into the marketplace, panting, with beads of sweat dotting his brow. The usually calm and carefree figure appeared flustered and distressed. A merchant took notice and inquired, 'Drukpa Nyonpa, what is it that is chasing you or you are chasing after? You are not your usual self today.'

Drukpa Kunley stopped abruptly and said, 'I've lost my doechag[77] and have failed to get it back.'

'How could you possibly lose your doechag so suddenly, and who might have taken it from you?' asked the merchant.

'Nyingmapas[78] have stolen it from me and renamed it zungma[79], claiming it as their own,' replied Drukpa Kunley. 'They now refuse to give it back.'

As Drukpa Kunley moved away, a few gomchens in a nearby stall exchanged knowing glances and remarked, 'The mad Drukpa is displeased with our taking of wives.' The merchant shook his head in amazement and smiled.

---

77 Desire or attachment
78 Followers of the Nyingma school
79 Spiritual consort

A week later, Drukpa Kunley suddenly came darting across the main street of Lhasa. He gasped for breath and looked distressed. A nomad bartering cheese and butter recognized him and inquired, 'Drukpa Nyonpa, what are you running away from? You appear unsettled today.'

'Nothing is pursuing me,' Drukpa Kunley replied, pausing to catch his breath. 'I'm pursuing something I've lost.'

'What have you lost?' asked the nomad, surprised, for he knew Drukpa Kunley had no material things to lose.

'My zhedang[80],' said Drukpa Kunley.

'But how?'

'Gelugpas[81] have stolen it from me and renamed it tshenyi[82], claiming it as their own,' said Drukpa Kunley. 'They now refuse to give it back.'

The nomad was perplexed. As Drukpa Kunley walked away, he turned to a nearby monk, who happened to be from the Kagyu school, and asked innocently, 'How could Gelugpas rename zhedang as tshenyi? The monk smiled pleasantly and explained that the Drukpa madman was alluding to the Gelug school's debating culture, which often turned rowdy and rancorous, causing aversion.

After that incident, Drukpa Kunley left Lhasa, wandering off to various corners of Tibet. He made every step count as training in mindfulness. He observed with keen interest how people practised dharma and how cultural and social habits affected authentic spiritual practice, and explored ways to preserve the primordial awareness of the mind.

---

80 Aversion
81 Followers of the Gelug school
82 Dialectics

Although he described his wanderings as aimless, Drukpa Kunley regarded every visit—whether to a religious site or a secular location—as a pilgrimage of sort. With each encounter and every place he visited, he strived to deepen his self-awareness. He said mindless pilgrimages were a waste of time, believing that the merit gained from such pilgrimages was not even enough to atone for the number of insects killed beneath one's feet.

During his travels, he made several stops at Kagyu and Sakya monasteries, keenly observing the seemingly devout practices of the resident monks. During his visits to Kagyu monasteries, he had observed monks purportedly meditating on the nature of the mind in the name of Mahamudra, only to succumb to slumber.

Upon his return to Lhasa, Drukpa Kunley hit the bustling marketplace once again, urgently looking for something he had lost. His reappearance in the market after weeks made everybody curious. As he darted through the busy streets, a curious pilgrim from Bhutan took note of his frantic pace and inquired, 'What have you lost, Naljorpa? I know you have no material possessions to lose.'

'My timug[83],' replied Drukpa Kunley.

'How could you suddenly lose your timug?' asked the pilgrim. 'It's not a tangible thing.'

'Even intangible things can be lost,' said Drukpa Kunley. 'Kagyupas[84] have stolen it from me and renamed it chagjachenpo[85], claiming it as their own. They now refuse to give it back.'

Amused murmurs rippled through the onlookers as the pilgrim chuckled. Observing the scene, a Kagyu monk approached the pilgrim, inquiring about the reason for laughter. 'Drukpa Kunley

---

83 Mental stupor
84 Followers of the Kagyu school
85 Mahamudra

alleges that his timug has been stolen by Kagyupas,' explained the pilgrim.

'This crazy Drukpa finds amusement in needling us whenever he can,' remarked the monk, turning away.

When Drukpa Kunley ventured into the marketplace the following day with an unusual sense of urgency, a vendor intercepted him and teased, 'Drukpa Nyonpa, what have you lost today? Another affliction, perhaps?' Onlookers gathered around Drukpa Kunley, anticipating a thought-provoking answer.

Pausing before the vendor, Drukpa Kunley replied, 'Yes indeed, I've lost ngagyal[86] today.'

'The thieves must be monks this time, too,' the vendor quipped.

'Yes, Sakyapas[87] have stolen it from me and renamed it lamdre[88], claiming it as their own,' said Drukpa Kunley. 'They now refuse to give it back.'

'How come Sakyapas?' asked the vendor.

'Because their perception of their own practice is lofty and vain, even self-defeating,' explained Drukpa Kunley.

As Drukpa Kunley turned to leave, having lost all his poisonous afflictive emotions to the monks of the four major schools of Buddhism, the marketplace of Lhasa paused for a while to reflect on his words. He then joined a group of musicians at a nearby street corner, immersing himself in the melodies of folk songs. Good music inspired in him the most authentic feelings and removed all self-doubt. It is the only enduring thing common to the disparate groups of practitioners like the enduring presence of the lofty mountains rising above Lhasa.

---

86 Pride
87 Followers of the Sakya school
88 Path and Fruit, the philosophical foundation of the Sakya school of Buddhism.

CHAPTER 28

The Farting Metaphysicist and Tsongkhapa

THE FARTING METAPHYSICIST AND TSONGKHAPA

One splendid morning in Lhasa, Drukpa Kunley awoke to the realization that he hadn't seen the god himself despite living in the abode of the gods, Lhasa. Driven by this realization, he immediately set out to meet Gyalwa Tsongkhapa[89], the hallowed incarnation of Jampalyang and the abbot of Ramoche Monastery which was situated in the northwest of Lhasa. He wanted to find out how Tsongkhapa, the founder of the Gelug school of Buddhism, lived his life.

The monks of Ramoche were taking on one another in a vigorous metaphysical debate when Drukpa Kunley arrived at the monastery. Barging in on them and saying he was also interested in a bit of metaphysics, he held out a fistful of fart under a monk's nose and asked, 'Tell me now, does smell come from air or air from smell?'

Enraged, the monks snapped at him that Ramoche was not a place for a madman's foolery. 'Wait, be patient,' Drukpa Kunley asserted. 'There's something different about the dharma you practise. My dharma quells the mind, yours agitates it.'

Everybody looked at him blankly, not knowing what to say before he asked them to take him to Tsongkhapa without dilly-dallying. The monks demanded that he produce a present for the abbot to meet him. 'I didn't know that I needed a present to see your abbot,' a surprised Drukpa Kunley said. 'Could I see the lama now and bring the present later?'

'Who in the world does that?' The monks mocked him.

'I have nothing on me right now except a pair of balls my parents gave me,' Drukpa Kunley retorted. 'Would they do?'

---

89 Drukpa Kunley was born only thirty-six years after Tsongkhapa's death. Geshe Gendün Rinchen seems to have reproduced a folktale in his biography of Drukpa Kunley.

Rudely taken aback again, the infuriated monks picked up sticks and chased him out of the monastery. The monks darted their angry eyes after him.

'I'll come back with a present and taunt them,' Drukpa Kunley thought as he walked away.

From there, Drukpa Kunley travelled to Samye in search of a present for Tsongkhapa.

One year later, a devotee couple insisted that he accept fifty sang[90] of gold and a piece of turquoise. He took the offering. Carrying the gold in his hands and the turquoise stuck in his penis hole, he hit the buzzing town of Lhasa, shouting, 'Buy turquoise if you like gold. Buy gold if you like turquoise.'

In front of the statue of Machig Palha[91] was a group of girls offering a song of praise to the goddess. They sang:

> She who dwells under the gilded golden dome,
> The Only Protector Mother, the Glorious Goddess.
> For you are endowed with the eye of wisdom,
> We, young girls, offer you songs of praise.

'Your song is melodious,' said Drukpa Kunley. 'Let me now sing my song.'

> In the glorious holy realm of Lhasa
> Before the Glorious Goddess, the Only Mother,
> Incense and butter lamps are offered every day.
> I, carefree Kunga Legpa, offer today
> The rare blend of penis and turquoise.
> Kindly accept it and hold us in your heart.

---

90 A unit of weight
91 Another name for deity Palden Lhamo

As he sang this song, the turquoise shot out of his penis hole and lodged itself on the forehead of Machig Palha.

After offering the turquoise to the statue, Drukpa Kunley went straight to Ramoche where the monks greeted him, 'We hope you aren't here this time to meet our lama with your pair of balls.'

'I have gold this time,' he said.

The monks' faces brightened up. 'Then you go straight in,' one of them declared. And in seconds, Drukpa Kunley found himself before Gyalwa Tsongkhapa, who sat on a high, decorated throne. Turning to the gold chest, Drukpa Kunley prayed:

> The Crown Jewel of Tibet's scholars, Tsongkhapa,
> Homage to you, the dispeller of mental darkness.
> He who is prophesied by Atisha, the holder of the white lotus[92],
> Homage to the bearer of the Three Vows, pure and sublime.
> He who holds the sword of wisdom on the utpala lotus[93],
> I pay homage to the teacher, debater and composer.
> He who is cloaked in a net of gold, unmatched in charisma,
> Homage to the dispeller of poverty and destitution.
>
> He who is delighted by a small chest of gold,
> Homage to the lover of worldly riches.
> He who could not be met in Ramoche last year,
> Homage to one who looks away from the poor.

Expressing pleasure tinged with embarrassment at Drukpa Kunley's outspoken criticism, Gyalwa Tsongkhapa gave him a

---

92 White lotus is the symbol of Chenrezig.
93 The sword of wisdom and utpala lotus are the symbols of Manjushri, the Bodhisattva of Wisdom.

knotted white scarf and acknowledged, 'You are right, Kunga Legpa, you are right! Take this, for you have no other needs.'

Pausing at the doorstep, Drukpa Kunley considered how he might carry the scarf. It was not at all comfortable around his neck. He did not have a pouch on his clothes to put it in, and his hands would not always be free to carry it. His penis, he concluded, was clean and it had nothing to carry.

So, he tied the scarf around his penis and marched into the heart of the marketplace, announcing, 'Look! Look, folks! If you can afford to offer fifty sang of gold, even the Omniscient One can be pleased to give you such a thing in return.'

The noisy town paused and fell silent for a while.

CHAPTER 29

Drukpa's Loud-voiced Friend

It was a usual day in Drepung Monastery, which was set against a barren hillside some distance west of Lhasa. The monastery complex reverberated with the sounds of horns and gongs. The monks darted across the vast courtyard carrying teapots and incense burners.

Everybody was frantically busy when Drukpa Kunley hit the courtyard at a leisurely pace and in an expansive mood. He was looking for the abbot.

Drukpa Kunley had come from Lhasa where he had spent a few days with his consort, Palzang Buthri. He wanted to mock the monks of Drepung.

'Who are you?' The abbot asked Drukpa Kunley, who had said he wished to join the monastery as a novice.

'I'm a Drukpa,' replied Drukpa Kunley.

'Hmm, Drukpa,' said the abbot, throwing his robe over his bare arms. 'Do you have a loud voice?'

'My voice is not particularly loud, but I have a friend whose voice is remarkably loud,' Drukpa Kunley replied, feigning a stentorian tone.

'Why don't you bring your friend in, then?' suggested the abbot.

As Drukpa Kunley walked across the prayer halls on his way out, he could hear the monks chanting in impossibly low, throaty voices that sounded almost like long horns. 'This is what the abbot meant,' he thought, smiling.

When the monks congregated the following morning, Drukpa Kunley brought in a donkey clad in a red robe, pulling it by the ear.

'What's this?' asked the abbot, grim-faced.

'This is my friend with a remarkably loud voice,' Drukpa Kunley replied with a mischievous grin. Then he slapped the donkey, which let out a deafening bray. The younger monks erupted in laughter while the older ones stared at the abbot quizzically.

As the abbot shooed the donkey away muttering to himself, Drukpa Kunley observed that instead of practising meditation, the monastery was emphasizing the loudness of voice as its dharma.

As Drukpa Kunley walked away from the monastery, the monks asked him, 'Where are you headed now, Drukpa Kunley?'

'Drukpa Kunley has nowhere to go and nowhere to stay,' he replied. 'Neither in the hell realm nor in Drepung is there a place for me.'

The monks giggled in amusement. 'Why is it so?' They asked him in a cacophony of voices.

'I've accumulated negative karma engaging in all manner of eccentric behaviour,' he explained. 'So, I decided to spend a few days in the hell realm. But the path to the hell realm is crowded by the monks of Sera Monastery.' The monks of Sera Monastery, founded in 1419 and one of the largest monasteries north of Lhasa, were the rivals of the monks of Drepung Monastery, founded in 1416. Gaden, Sera and Drepung were among the biggest Gelug monasteries in Tibet.

The monks guffawed and slapped one another on the back. 'So, you came back?' they asked impatiently.

'So, I came back and decided to join Drepung Monastery,' he continued. 'But Drepung is filled with jealousy, attachment and aversion. There's no place for me here either.'

As laughter disappeared from the noisy monks, Drukpa Kunley disappeared from their sight.

CHAPTER 30

The Miracle Behind Trashi Lhunpo's Famed Tea

Tsechen Monastery in southern Tibet was spectacularly located on a hilltop commanding the view of Gyangtse and surrounding valleys. It was among the biggest monasteries in Tibet and home to three hundred monks.

Today, the fourteenth century Sacha monastery was bustling with the monks performing their bimonthly sojong, the healing and purification ritual to atone for the violation of monastic vows. The assembly hall reverberated with the sonorous prayers chanted by the monks sitting in straight rows.

Servers shuffled across the long hallways carrying huge kettles and bowls. Devotees from the nearby villages arrived with backloads of butter and tea. The storekeeper took their offerings and took down their names. A load of butter was immediately taken to the kitchen for a round of butter tea for the monks.

Among the stream of devotees was a self-assured man with a carefree demeanour. He offered a morsel of tea in a cup the size of a yak's eye and said, 'Can you brew special tea for the monks with this?'

The monks looked curiously at the man and said, 'This morsel is not enough for three hundred monks.'

The man, Drukpa Kunley, smiled and stepped aside. He neither looked like any of the monks at the monastery nor like any of the herders who came to make their offerings. But he carried himself with enigmatic confidence, charm and grace.

'Let me give them a dose of their own medicine,' he thought. On his way out, he jumped over boulders and walked around small rocks.

'Look how this madman walks!' said bemused monks to one another.

'This is how you practise your dharma,' said Drukpa Kunley mockingly.

'Our dharma has no such practice,' rebutted the monks, laughing. 'It must be madmen's practice.'

'Do you know how your practice is like how I walked?' retorted Drukpa Kunley. 'Buddha's Vinaya underlines four primary vows and abstinence from alcohol as essential, while the breach of subsidiary vows can be atoned for. You disregard the primary vows and focus your attention on subsidiary vows with unnecessary seriousness by observing rituals such as sojong. You'd better think about it.'

From Tsechen, Drukpa Kunley went to Gangchen Chophel Monastery in Tsang. There, too, his tea offering was rejected and he was turned away.

Undeterred, he proceeded to Trashi Lhunpo Monastery founded by the first Dalai Lama in 1447, the traditional seat of Panchen Lama and one of the four principal monasteries of the Gelug school of Buddhism. Six thousand monks filled the great assembly hall of the monastery.

He met the discipline master and offered to serve tea to the assembly of monks. The discipline master was anything but convinced by the amount of tea Drukpa Kunley handed him but gave him the benefit of doubt. He consulted the abbot who said Drukpa Kunley was a great siddha, so he might be allowed to do whatever he wished.

Drukpa Kunley dropped his handful of tea leaves and an egg-sized ball of butter into the monastic kitchen's colossal copper cauldron. He threw the lid over the pot and instructed the monks not to lift it until he returned from the marketplace.

He went to a tavern in the marketplace where he treated himself to a large quantity of chang and flirted with girls.

Meanwhile, the discipline master grew increasingly anxious. There might not be tea for the monks. At tea time, he blew his conch shell to gather the monks and announced, 'I'm afraid we will have to settle for hot water today. A Drukpa has promised us tea but he is gone and has not returned to check on his tea.'

However, when the lid was lifted, the cauldron was almost full with richly brewed tea.

Just then, Drukpa Kunley dashed in. Seeing that the lid had been taken off the cauldron, he declared that the cauldron could never be filled beyond that level in the future. The tea made from a handful of tea leaves and a small lump of butter turned out to be thick, buttery, delicious, and more than enough for six thousand monks. Thanks to that auspicious occurrence, Trashi Lhunpo is famed for its delicious tea to this day.

'The monks must be served chang now,' Drukpa Kunley proposed. The discipline master objected that chang was not permissible. But Drukpa Kunley insisted that his chang was indispensable to make the occasion auspicious. So, he had his way once again.

He walked to the centre of the assembly hall, broke wind thunderously and announced, 'Please accept my offering of chang now.' The young novices chuckled in amusement while the older monks covered their nose. The gas permeated the hall with a pleasant smell.

To this day, the young novices of Trashi Lhunpo are known for exuding a characteristic pleasant odour that weakens as they age.

CHAPTER 31
No Place is Safe without Self-restraint

When Drukpa Kunley started wandering across Tibet, he was fully convinced that he could not practise the dharma confined to one place. He realized that lingering in one place for long often led to attachment to the place and patrons. It fostered a sense of competition for the respect of laypeople.

Liberated from filial and institutional ties, he wandered freely as a mendicant, traversing the vast expanse of the country. He was nineteen years old at that time. In his wanderings, he encountered illustrious lamas from whom he received essential teachings. He took novice vows from the abbot of Nenying and full ordination vows from Khyen Rabpa of Zhalu Monastery who named him Kunga Legpa Paljor Zangpo.

His travels led him to numerous monastic schools, where he crossed paths with practitioners of varying calibre. He engaged them in spirited scriptural and philosophical debates and sang stirring dharma songs whenever they requested him. Recurring themes in his songs included 'loving others more than oneself'[94] and 'abandoning the material needs of life'[95]. He said that a dharma practitioner must 'offer gain and victory to others and take loss and defeat for oneself'.[96] Otherwise, the practitioner is simply a layperson in religious robes.

During one of his travels, he met a renunciant from Nepal who drank chang and said it was permissible for a practitioner as long as it was drunk without getting attached to it. Drukpa Kunley found his logic problematic. He observed, 'Detachment is indeed a hallmark of yogis. Yet, is it acceptable to kill, steal, cheat

---

94 བདག་བས་གཞན་གཅེས།
95 ཚེ་འདིའི་བློ་ཡིས་སྟོངས།
96 ཁེ་དང་རྒྱལ་ཁ་གཞན་ལ་སྒྱིན། གྱོང་དང་ཕམ་ཁ་རང་གིས་འཁུར།

and prepare and serve poison if one remains unattached to the act itself?'

The renunciant, caught off guard, mumbled a hesitant reply, his fingers tightening around his chang cup.

Drukpa Kunley was about to leave, but turned back to say, 'If you say deities and dharma protectors drink amrita, which is a form of chang, do they buy this chang? Do they brew it? What substance is it made from? Why would they, whose bodies are like rainbows, need alcohol? If one could eliminate all discursive thoughts, there is no difference between chang and water. As long as craving for chang persists, all justifications for drinking it are flimsy.'

The Nepali renunciant squirmed in his seat and wrung his hands. He stammered, searching for a retort, but words failed him. Before he could muster a response, Drukpa Kunley turned and disappeared down the dusty path with a playful smile.

As he ambled off towards Daglha Gampo—a Kagyu monastery in the southern reaches of Tibet founded by the renowned disciple of Milarepa, Gampopa (1079–1153) in the year 1121—a scene of devout practice unfolded before him. Monks, nuns, gomchens, and lay devotees were engaged in a fasting ritual, chanting mani and prostrating like waves.

Unnoticed by anyone, Drukpa Kunley positioned himself in a secluded corner and started chanting the following verse:

Homage to the unseen blissful body of sambhogakaya
Homage to the unborn and unceasing body of dharmakaya
Homage to the omnipresent manifestation of nirmanakaya

Homage to all lamas if they bear the mark of perfection
Homage to all deities if they grant wishes and blessings
Homage to all dakinis if they fulfill their virtuous deeds

> Homage to all dharma protectors if they clear obstacles
> Homage to all teachings if they are vast and profound
> Homage to all practitioners if they are noble and virtuous

> Homage to all views if they are free and limitless
> Homage to all meditation if it is free of references
> Homage to all conduct if it is free of hypocrisy

Even as the devotees extolled the profundity of his impromptu prayer that reflected the fertility of his mind, Drukpa Kunley slipped into his signature ribald and irreverent humour.

> Homage to the ear of the leader that refuses to hear petitions
> Homage to the mind of the servant that refuses to take orders

> Homage to the mouth of the rich that refuses to eat enough
> Homage to the wealth of the poor that refuses to increase

> Homage to the married man who drifts after mistresses
> Homage to the tongue of the crooked that spins falsehood

> Homage to the ear that rejects old wisdom for young chatter
> Homage to the vagina of the old woman that defies death

> Homage to the children who pay back kindness with malice
> Homage to the body in monastic robes without the three vows

'He is truly mad,' some people observed.
'He is a great prattler,' others remarked, laughing.

Chenga Rinpoche, the revered hierarch of Daglha Gampo, intervened and said they had misunderstood Drukpa Kunley, a great yogi who had transcended all dualistic perceptions. 'He is neither mad, nor foolish,' he told them. 'You must now beg for his forgiveness.'

All monks, nuns, gomchens, and laypeople gathered at the monastery prostrated to Drukpa Kunley and begged for forgiveness. But he stood unfazed, neither feeling ridiculed nor respected. Instead, he broke into a moving song.

Once he had completed the song, Chenga Rinpoche, intrigued by Drukpa Kunley's endless wanderings, inquired about his experiences and encounters. In response, Drukpa Kunley offered a song that encapsulated numerous places he had been to and people he had encountered.

> I, the Naljorpa, did not linger in one place. I, the Naljorpa, went wandering. I, the Naljorpa, visited the monasteries of the Kagyu school. In those monasteries, each monk held a pitcher of chang. Fearing I might get involved in the transaction of chang as a singer, I, the Naljorpa, restrained myself.
>
> I, the Naljorpa, visited the monasteries of the Sacha school. In those monasteries, all monks showed contempt for all religious doctrines. Fearing I might get involved in the act of forsaking the dharma, I, the Naljorpa, restrained myself.
>
> I, the Naljorpa, visited the monasteries of the Gedan school. In those monasteries, monks were consumed by attachment and aversion. Fearing I might become a biased dharma practitioner, I, the Naljorpa, restrained myself.
>
> I, the Naljorpa, visited Zolphu Monastery. In that monastery, senior monks were self-seeking. Fearing I might become the robber of alms beggars, I, the Naljorpa, restrained myself.
>
> I, the Naljorpa, visited the Nyingma school of tantrikas. In that school, practitioners expected blessings from mask dances.

Fearing I might become a ritual dancer and dark meditator, I, the Naljorpa, restrained myself.

I, the Naljorpa, visited mountain hermitages of past masters. In those hermitages, worldly affairs were the order of the day. Fearing retribution from the Three Jewels, I, the Naljorpa, restrained myself.

I, the Naljorpa, visited cemeteries and secluded hermitages. In those cemeteries and hermitages, Chod practitioners sought name and fame. Fearing I might become friends with worldly gods and demons, I, the Naljorpa, restrained myself.

I, the Naljorpa, visited people who built religious structures and encouraged dharma activities. Most of those people consumed items of offerings as food. Fearing I might become a compulsive liar, I, the Naljorpa, restrained myself.

I, the Naljorpa, went to meet renunciants who make pilgrimages. Those pilgrims visiting sacred sites delighted in material possessions more than meditation. Fearing I might become a profit-seeking trader, I, the Naljorpa, restrained myself.

I, the Naljorpa, visited the Drukpa monastery. In that monastery, internal disputes raged between natives and foreigners. Fearing I might get embroiled in a family dispute, I, the Naljorpa, restrained myself.

I, the Naljorpa, visited practitioners undergoing years or a lifetime of retreat. Those practitioners were simply counting their days. Fearing I might become the guard of a retreatant's little hut, I, the Naljorpa, restrained myself.

I, the Naljorpa, went to meet lamas. Those lamas were engrossed in worldly affairs. Fearing I might turn into an unruly monk, I, the Naljorpa, restrained myself.

I, the Naljorpa, went to meet lamas' attendants. Those attendants were toiling in servitude for their lamas. Fearing I might become the servant of a lama's attendant, I, the Naljorpa, restrained myself.

I, the Naljorpa, visited places where adepts practised. In those places, adepts were offensive to gods, demons and humans. Fearing I might become offensive and vindictive to them all, I, the Naljorpa, restrained myself.

I, the Naljorpa, went to meet rich people. The mournful cry of those rich people was louder than that of hell. Fearing I might be reborn as spirit Apara, I, the Naljorpa, restrained myself.

I, the Naljorpa, went to meet shameless beggars. Those beggars had squandered their ancestral property. Fearing I might become a disgrace to everyone, I, the Naljorpa, restrained myself.

I, the Naljorpa, visited the monasteries of great meditators. In those monasteries, each great meditator had a spiritual consort. Fearing I might become a householder tantric monk, I, the Naljorpa, restrained myself.

I, the Naljorpa, visited the monasteries of philosophers. In those monasteries, each philosopher had a novice as a sexual companion. Fearing I might commit the moral violation of sexual intercourse, I, the Naljorpa, restrained myself.

I, the Naljorpa, visited the sacred place of Lhasa. In Lhasa, there was a guest for each tea house. Fearing I might become the cleaner of Kyidzom, I, the Naljorpa, restrained myself.

I, the Naljorpa, visited all countries in all directions. In all those countries, everyone was self-absorbed. Fearing I might develop the view of shravakas[97] and pratyeka-buddhas[98], I, the Naljorpa, restrained myself.

'How about your dharma practice?' someone inquired of Drukpa Kunley.

'Well,' replied Drukpa Kunley with humility. 'I've always aspired to understand everything—from the enlightened state of the Buddha all the way down to the depths of the hell realm. I excel at reading and comprehending scriptures. However, my practice has long been tainted by the allure of the eight worldly concerns[99].'

---

[97] Shravakas are disciples who seek enlightenment for their own benefit and liberation from the cycle of birth and death (samsara).

[98] Also known as 'solitary realizers' or 'self-enlightened ones', pratyeka-buddhas attain enlightenment through their own efforts but do not actively teach others.

[99] The eight worldly concerns (འཇིག་རྟེན་ཆོས་བརྒྱད་) are mundane concerns that motivate the actions of ordinary human beings. In pairs, they are: hope for pleasure and fear of pain, hope for gain and fear of loss, hope for praise and fear of criticism, hope for good reputation and fear of bad reputation.

CHAPTER 32

When a Snobbish Family Saw Excrement for Tormas

'I will go ahead and prepare the tormas[100],' proposed Drukpa Kunley.

'That would save me a lot of time,' said Lama Ngawang Chogyal, who had been invited to preside over an annual religious ritual in a wealthy household in Drakpisa village of Punakha. 'But make sure you conduct yourself properly.'

'Rest assured, I can take care of myself,' assured Drukpa Kunley as he stood up to leave. He walked away unsteadily, swinging his arms wildly. From a distance, he turned around and joked, 'I hope the family has no young daughters to distract me.'

Lama Ngawang Chogyal frowned and sighed disapprovingly. He was a regular target of Drukpa Kunley's ridicule for his conventional notions of morality conditioned by religious institutions. The cousins' notions of morality, particularly chastity, and way of life were polar opposites. Lama Ngawang Chogyal was ten years younger than Drukpa Kunley.

Early on the day of the ritual, as Drukpa Kunley knocked on the door of the house, the family members were surprised to find that their high lama had sent a seemingly destitute person to make the tormas for the grand ritual. From that moment, they saw him doing everything in a bizarre manner. His appearance fluctuated from moment to moment. One moment, he looked like a beggar; the next moment, he looked like a monk and the next, he looked like a hunter. The family doubted if Lama Ngawang Chogyal had sent the right person ahead of him.

Once seated inside, Drukpa Kunley drank several pots of chang before asking for flour, butter, sugar and chang to make dough for the tormas. 'His speciality is chang, not torma,' the family members whispered to each other.

---

100 Ritual cakes

As Drukpa Kunley kneaded the dough and started making the tormas, the family saw him devouring the dough. They assumed that the beggar was famished. The family was distressed by the weird scenes that were unfolding. They were worried that there would be no tormas for the altar when the high lama would arrive. However, they could not bring themselves to question Drukpa Kunley due to his strangely imposing personality.

Towards the afternoon, with the lama expected soon, Drukpa Kunley began laying out the tormas on the altar tastefully. To their shock, the family saw him squatting on the altar and defecating. The altar was soon filled with rows of fresh, steaming conical excrement—a big cone in the centre flanked by smaller, neatly arranged cones. The pungent smell of human excrement permeated the whole house forcing the family to rush out with their noses and mouths covered.

As Lama Ngawang Chogyal arrived riding a pony, the family was exasperated. 'Our house is thoroughly polluted and defiled by human excrement,' they informed the lama. 'You won't be able to come in before we clean up the whole mess.'

To the family's surprise, the lama was unfazed by the disgusting scene they described. He knew these were Drukpa Kunley's antics. He smiled and said, 'There is nothing to worry about. Everything will be fine.'

As the family ushered the lama in, Drukpa Kunley sprinkled the holy water over the rows of excrement, miraculously transforming them into colourful tormas. At the same time, the house was filled with the aroma of incense, sweet and butter.

Before the family could apologize, Drukpa Kunley escaped through the window. The once-wealthy family dwindled and disappeared gradually, because of the inauspicious occurence.

The following day, Drukpa Kunley ascended the mountains overlooking the village and came back in hot pursuit of a sambar deer. As the villagers gathered to witness the intriguing scene, he swiftly brought the deer down with his arrow. As they watched in amazement, Drukpa Kunley asked them to partake in the consumption of the freshly killed deer's 'hot' meat and 'hot' blood. Everybody backed off except a man from the family of Amorimo. Cupping his palms, he drank a mouthful of the deer's blood from its carcass.

'This is an auspicious sign,' proclaimed Drukpa Kunley, prophesying that the man's descendants would become the ancestors of a distinguished reincarnation of a Buddhist saint instrumental in the propagation of dharma in Bhutan. That man's household has since remained the lineage home of the Jamgon Trulku, descendants of Drubthob Terkhungpa, a Tibetan Drukpa yogi. Today, Jamgon Trulku Mipham Chokyi Nyenjeth, born in 1983, stands as the sixth incarnation of the Jamgon lineage.

CHAPTER 33

To Earn the Worth of Ponies and Pussies

It was a pleasant day in Jiligang village of Punakha district in western Bhutan. Thousands of devotees had transformed the place into a meadow of multi-coloured dresses. Seated on a high throne facing the colourful crowd was the radiant Lama Ngawang Chogyal. The village elders had invited him from Ralung in Tibet. He was about to confer the long-life empowerment[101] to the village.

In the midst of this sacred ceremony, a scantily-clad man came along with a beautiful, well-adorned woman and a hunting dog. Everybody recognized him as Drukpa Kunley. He walked straight to the colourful throne and told the lama that he would serve the holy water without a vase. His dull figure was a contrast against the lavish, brocade-covered throne. He then turned to the devotees and announced loudly that they should close their eyes and stretch their hands to receive the holy water.

He held the shaft of his penis with the right hand and dripped his urine into each palm. Some lapped it up and praised its soothing taste; some flung their hand in disgust, saying they had been served penis water instead of holy water. The latter group of devotees was believed to have caused water scarcity in Jiligang.

As Lama Ngawang Chogyal conferred his empowerment, Drukpa Kunley stood by with his consort Adzom, kissing her, fondling her breasts, and displaying all kinds of sexual gestures.

That night, as Drukpa Kunley contemplated where the winter residence of his descendants would be, he saw a host of one thousand fire spirits congregated on top of the opposite hill. He threw a piece of burning wood into the congregation, scorching

---

101 It is a ritual that bestows blessings for health, vitality, and longevity.

all the spirits to death. The whole area was filled with the smell of burning meat. Lama Ngawang Chogyal noticed this.

The following morning, Lama Ngawang Chogyal was not pleased with Drukpa Kunley. He told his cousin, 'I know what you were up to last night. You sent the smell of roasted pork thick and fast into the air charged with spiritual energy.'

Drukpa Kunley explained what he was actually up to but his cousin was not convinced. 'Kunley, if you are always up to such mischief, don't follow me tomorrow to Gontoe where I've been invited,' he admonished Drukpa Kunley, 'you will only bring shame and indignity.'

'All right,' said Drukpa Kunley.

~

A huge crowd had gathered in Gontoe. A colourful, high throne had been planted on the ground. Lama Ngawang Chogyal was expected to arrive any moment.

Drukpa Kunley was already in the crowd, though. As the burbling noise of the crowd turned into hushed whispers at the sight of Lama Ngawang Chogyal, Drukpa Kunley quickly hopped onto the throne and started enacting all kinds of childish behaviours.

'I told you not to follow me here,' an irritated Lama Ngawang Chogyal said.

'You're right,' said Drukpa Kunley, 'that's why I have come here ahead of you.'

'Be gone after performing libation and drinking your share,' said Lama Ngawang Chogyal.

After performing libation, Drukpa Kunley disappeared from the scene, saying, 'I'm off to meet my Adzom. Better earn the worth of your ponies and my pussies from this ceremony.'

At midday, when the empowerment ceremony was in full swing, the sound of a barking dog could be heard. As the sound came closer, a stag came galloping into the crowd and lay down beside the lama's throne. The astonished devotees extolled the incident as a religious wonderment wrought by their lama. Drukpa Kunley caught up and shot the stag, saying, 'You should be up and running, not lying here.'

The empowerment ceremony continued; so did Drukpa Kunley's antics. He cut off the stag's head, skinned the carcass and cut it into small pieces. Then he roasted the meat, ate his share, and distributed the rest amongst the devotees.

The devotees were appalled. They were not able to take in what was happening. Lama Ngawang Chogyal was agitated by the bloody affair. When the whole carcass had been consumed, Drukpa Kunley gathered all the bare bones and piled them up. At the snap of his fingers, the bones turned into a live stag that fled into the mountains.

All eyes turned to Lama Ngawang Chogyal, who was unimpressed but visibly uneasy. Then, all eyes turned to Drukpa Kunley, who was beaming like the afternoon sun that had begun to cast long rays over the crowd.

At long last, Lama Ngawang Chogyal spoke from his throne, 'If a fellow like you, who survives on chang and girls, can resurrect a stag, there surely must be some remnant of spiritual realization from your past lives in you. If you claim mastery of ultimate accomplishments and magical powers, do it this way.' He removed his upper robe and flung it onto a sunbeam. The robe hung from the sunbeam, which bent slightly.

Drukpa Kunley let out a hearty guffaw and said, 'Wow, this is a remarkable feat accomplished by a man who wraps his penis tight and bears the burden of people's expectations on a throne. This is how you do it.' He threw his dog, bow and arrows onto another sunbeam which stretched straight and taut.

'How is it possible in spite of your much heavier weight?' asked Lama Ngawang Chogyal, surprised.

Drukpa Kunley replied, 'We are equals in terms of detachment and realization, but you are burdened by sensual trappings and worldly wealth.'

Then, Lama Ngawang Chogyal proposed, 'The spring is here, and it's becoming hot here. The two of us must return to Tibet.'

'You may go ahead,' Drukpa Kunley said. 'The voluptuous bottoms of the Bhutanese girls hold me back. I'll attend to them for about a year before returning home like an old bird to a roost, tired of ceaseless roaming.'

Epilogue

Some people love the spacious celestial realm,
Some people love the wealth of nagas,
May god lovers and naga lovers bring good luck.
Some people rejoice in the fruit of righteous deeds,
Some people rejoice in illusory wealth,
May peace seekers and misery seekers bring good luck.
Lord Ngawang Chogyal loves ponies,
I, Carefree Kunley, love pussies,
May the pony lover and pussy lover bring good luck.
Attendant Lekshey enjoys chang,
Palzang Dorji relishes meat,
May the meat eater and chang drinker bring good luck.
Chobchob Kharel revels in dice games,
Azhang Chungchab delights in singing,
May the dice player and singer bring good luck.
Baleb Zungzung enjoys chanting mani,
Dondub Palzang loves eating fish,
May the love of the dharma and fish bring good luck.
Ani Atsun likes to sleep,
Apa Achap likes to rise,
May the indolent and industrious bring good luck.
Toepa Tshewang loves the dharma,
Carefree Kunley loves the hostess,

May the dharma lover and hostess lover bring good luck.
Tsunchung Tashi loves Tibet,
Tsondru Zangmo loves Bhutan,
May the Tibet lover and Bhutan lover bring good luck.
Bearing a hero's strength matching strong chang,
Wearing fine clothes matching bejewelled hands,
May gallant young men bring good luck.
With a taste for fine ornaments and lust for good food,
A hearty appetite for good sex and fertility for good sons,
May fair maidens bring good luck.
The dharma that is taught and the ear that listens,
The goal that is set and teaching that is practised,
May teachers and disciples bring good luck.
The path and the comrades along the path,
The destination at the end of the path,
May the Triple Gem bring good luck.

Translated from Geshe Gendün Rinchen's *The Essence of a Sea of Biography of Drukpa Kunley that is Meaningful to Behold* (འབྲུག་པ་ཀུན་ལེགས་ཀྱི་རྣམ་ཐར་རྒྱ་མཚོའི་སྙིང་པོ་མཐོང་བ་དོན་ལྡན་) These are the last lines of the biography seeking good luck from all shades of life and living.

Acknowledgements

My profound fascination with Drukpa Kunley has inspired me to read his stories written in Choekey, a language beyond the reach of most people. As I immersed myself in his extraordinary tales, I began retelling them in modern English, making them accessible and appealing to contemporary readers.

Much shorter versions of the stories in this collection were written as far back as 2013. The process of crafting these narratives, often spaced five to six months apart, led me to a humbling realization about my limited knowledge of language, literature, history, folklore and creative writing.

Any quality this book may contain is due to the unwavering encouragement of numerous individuals who commended my attempts at writing and urged me to continue whenever I lost interest and paused for months. Among them, I am immensely grateful to the following individuals who generously shared their knowledge, time and motivation:

- To Lopen Kunzang Thinley, Dorji Gyeltshen, Rinchen Yoezer and Rinchen Dorji, who guided me whenever I encountered uncertainties regarding Choekey expressions and Buddhist concepts. I extend my deepest gratitude to Lopen Kunzang Thinley in particular for his exceptional kindness in sharing advice and encouragement.

- To Francoise Pommaret (PhD), Aum Tashi Pem, Tashi Dorji, Choki Wangmo and Jigme Wangchuk for their invaluable comments and feedback on the first draft of the manuscript.
- To Khenpo Phuntsho Tashi, Tandin Dorji (PhD), Bunty Avieson (PhD), Tshering Tashi, and my teacher Thakur S. Powdyel for their encouragement and feedback on the first draft of the manuscript.
- To my dear friend Chimi R. Namgyal, whose exquisite artistry breathes life into the colourful Drukpa Kunley, capturing his spirit in every stroke.
- To His Eminence Gyelsay Chogtrul Rinpoche for his kind words of encouragement and thoughtful foreword to the book.
- To Namita Gokhale, whose guidance placed the manuscript in the most fitting hands.
- To Lopen Karma Phuntsho (PhD) for his introduction to the book, which sets the perfect tone for the stories within these pages.
- To the talented editorial and design teams at HarperCollins, whose expertise has transformed the manuscript into this beautiful book.

In addition, I extend my gratitude to my family and numerous friends and colleagues for their wholehearted support and encouragement.

Index

abbot, 64, 90–94, 147, 152–153, 156, 159
abstinence, 156
Ache Palzang, 101
Adzom. *See* Gontoe Ache Adzom
Adzoma, 127, 131, 133
Afflictive emotions, 140, 143, 145
Age of five degenerations, 84
alcohol, xviii, xxi–xxii, xxvii–xxviii, 156, 160, *see also* chang, drinks
Ama, 18
Anan Dhara, 53
Angay Akyi, 27
Angdar, xxxv, 5, 110
Ani Atsun, 176
Ani Samten Palmo, 36–37
Ani Tshewang Palzom, 79–81
Apa, 50, 176
Apara, 164
Ardussi, John, xiii
arrows, xvii, 13–14, 34, 53, 69, 174
ascetic, xi
Atisha Dipamkara, 92, 149
attachment, 84, 102, 125, 142, 153, 159, 162
Autobiography of Great Yogi Kunga Legpa, xxxiii

Avalokiteshvara. *See* Chenrezig
avarice, 121, 123–125
Azhang Chungchab, 175

Baleb Zungzung, 175
Barbi Chozom. *See* Wangza Chozom
Bhrikuti, Princess, 137
Bhutan (Lhomon/Southern Mon), xi, 2, 4, 9–10, 14, 70
Bhutanese, xi–xii, xvi–xvii, xix–xx, xxii, xxx, xxxiv, 9, 16, 54, 63
biographies: Buddhist, xxxvii; of Drukpa Kunley, xvi, xxxiii–xxxiv
Biography of Drukpa Kunley Including His Deeds in Mon Paro Mipham Tshewang Tenzin, xxxiii
The Biography of Lord Kunga Lekpa Including His Deeds in Mon Paro, Tshewang Tenzin, xvi
blue sheep, 5, 127–128
Bodhisattva, xxxvi, 4, 9, 59, 75, 122, 149
bow, 113

Buddha, 4, 6, 61, 63, 73, 93, 128, 131, 133–134, 137; dharma, xxvi; nature, xxiii, 140; Vinaya of, 156; within, xxvi, 75
Buddhahood, 84, 140
Buddhism, xx–xxi, xxvi, 63, 68–69, 145, 147, 156; to Bhutan, xii; Tibetan, xix, 66n54, 101
Buddhist Digital Resource Centre, xiii
bull, 39–40, 42, 52–61
Bumthang, xiv, 29, 67–70, 72
byatang (carefree vagrant), xi

Chagkhar, 69
Chagkhar Gyalpo, 69
Chang, xxv–xxvi, xxxii, 4, 22–24, 26, 35, 42, 68–70, 83–85, 87–88, 97–98, 110, 114, 156–157, 159–160, 162, 167, 175–176
Chenga Rinpoche, 161–162
Chenrezig, 9, 51, 149
Cheri, 7
Chobchob Kharel, 175
Chod, 88, 163
Chodrak Gyatsho, Seventh Karmapa, xxxvi, 102
Chodrak Gyatso, seventh Karmapa, xiv
Choechong Kyi, *see* Longrong Dudmo
Choekey, xxxiv–xxxv, xxxvii, 46
Chogden Gonpo, 73
choje (religious lord), xi, 73
Choje Kunley, 73
Choje Ngawang Chogyal, 125

Chungsey Ache Gyalzom, 53
Chuyur, in Paro, 5, 17, 21
clairvoyance, 54; Angay was going to die, 24; donkey is your lama, 106; Karmapa has lost his mental vow, 101; right location for the toilet, 76
cliffs, residences of powerful rock spirits, xx
Compassion, 9, 47, 72, 75; absence of self-love, 58; loving others more than oneself, 159
consort, xxxii, 41, 46–47, 71, 98, 142, 152, 164, 171
conventions, xvi, xviii
corruption, xviii, xxiii
crazy-wisdom master, xvi, xviii
creative, xxxiv, xxxvii
cremation ground, 25, 27–28
customs, xxiv

Dagala, 36
Dalai Lama, first, 156
Dardang Goechen Mentsi Drolma, 111
Deb Morong. *See* Tsang Desi
Deeds of Lam Drukpa Kunley, xxxiii
demon, xvii, xx, 11, 35, 46, 163–164; hungry, 34; of Toep Lungdram Wogma, 3, 5–6; of Wang Gonsakha, 34, 36–37; of Wodod Drak, 10
demonesses, 12–14, 29, 45; of Dochula, 39–40; of Hinglila, 40; Longrong Dudmo, 44,

46–47; Shingkarab, 13; of Singlila, 40; of Toebisa, 40
dependent origination, xxviii; few people and few corpses, xxix, 31; phallus-shaped weed, xxix; wealthy family dwindled, 168
detachment, xxviii, 159, 174
devotion, 22–24, 49, 55, 61, 68, 70, 86, 131
dharma, xxvi–xxvii, xxxi, 6–7, 58, 61, 83, 85–87, 111, 138, 153, 155, 162; activities, 163; language, xxxiv; lord, 70; path, 44; practice, 165; practitioners, 93, 159; and propagation, 2; protectors, 2, 37, 47, 160–161; teachers, xxvii
Dharmakaya Samantabhadra, 71
Divine Madman, The, xvii, xxxiv
Dochula, 3, 5, 38–41
Dochula Pass, 39
doechag (desire), xxxvi, 45, 47–48, 56, 68, 85, 90, 103, 109, 120, 142
dog/dogs, 86, 114, 117, 119, 122–123
Dog Year, 98
Dondrub Zangmo, 42
donkey, 104; clad in a red robe, 152; incarnate, 104–105, 107; lama born as a donkey, 106; in leopard's skin, 84; shed a torrent of tears, 106
Donyo Dorje, Rinpungpa ruler, xiv
Dorgong, xxxv

Dorji Lingpa, 73
Dowman, Keith, xvii, xxxiv
Drakpisa, 167
drinks, xxxii
drubthob. *See* saint
Drubthob Terkhungpa, 169
Drukgyal, 5
Druk Nyon, 140, (*see also* Druk Nyon Kunley, Drukpa, Drukpa Kunley, Drukpa Nyonpa, Druk Nyon Kunga Legpa, Jatang Kunley, Kunga Legpa); autobiography, xviii, xxxiv–xxxv; childhood, xiii, xxxi; distinguished lineage, xxix; family, xiii–xiv, xxii, xxix, xxxi, 7, 24, 30–31, 42, 50, 163, 166–169; physical appearance, xxxiv; secret biography, xxxiiin17; various names, xxvn1
Druk Nyon Kunga Legpa, 96, 98, 138
Druk Nyon Kunley, 81
Drukpa, xi–xii
Drukpa Kagyu, xi–xii, xxx, 2, 7, 90
Drukpa Kunley, 175; birth of, xiii, xxxi; Divine Madman Drukpa Kunley, xxxi; dream of, 2; as Druknyon or 'Madman of Druk,' xi, xv; as Drukpa Kagyu master, xxx; as endowed priest, xviii; Holy Madman of Druk, 11; master of magical power, xvii; as patron saint of Bhutan,

xii; popularity of, xvii; sexual
relations, xxxv–xxxvi; stories
of, xvii, xxii–xxiv; vagabond,
xiv; to women planting paddy,
xxix
Drukpa Ngawang Chogyal, 64
Drukpa Nyonpa, 142–143, 145
Drung Drung Gyalzom, 29n39
drunkard, xi
Duezhi, xxxii
duplicity, xxvii, 86
Dzogchen, 71
Dzombu Kyi, dharma protector,
47
Dzongkha, xxxiii–xxxiv, xxxvii

empowerment ceremony, 101,
124, 173
enlightened, xv, xvii, xx–xxi
enlightenment, xvii–xviii, 75, 135,
140, 165
*The Essence of a Sea of Biography
of Drukpa Kunley That is
Meaningful to Behold*, Gendün
Rinchen, xvi, xxxiii

fertility, xxi, 161
folktales, xxxiii–xxxiv, 9
forests, as haunts of gods and
demons, xx
Fourth Druk Desi or temporal
ruler of Bhutan, 7

Gaden, 105, 127–129, 153
Gadra, 96, 98–99
Gadrawa, 96–97, 99

Gampopa, 160
Gasa. *See* Gon
Gelugpas, 143
Gelug school, 143, 147, 156
Gendün Rinchen, sixty-ninth Je
Khenpo of Bhutan, xvi
generosity, 58, 60
Gene Smith, E., xiii
genitals, 5; phallus (penis), xxxiv,
11, 33–34, 40, 56, 61, 110,
148, 150, 171, 173; scrotums,
14, 61; vaginas, xxxiv, xxxvi,
36, 48, 56, 59, 110, 161
Geshe Gendün Rinchen, 147n91;
biography of Drukpa Kunley,
xxxiv
Geynyen Jagpa Melen, 90
girls, xxv–xxvi, 4, 14, 53–54,
56–60, 68, 70, 79, 81,
101–103, 132, 148, 173–174;
choice of, xxxv–xxxvi; in
dream, 2; of Gyangtse, 130,
133–134; liberation of, xxxv;
Palden Lhamo as, 2; Sacha,
108–109, 111; spiritually
inclined, xxxvi
goat, 52–61
Goat-headed bull. *See* takin
Goddess Tara, 134
gods, xx, 46, 63, 88, 147, 164
gomchens, 83, 142, 160, 162
Gon (Gasa), xxx, xxxviii
Gonsakha, 5, 34, 36–37
Gontoe, 172
Gontoe Ache Adzom, 53,
171–172

INDEX

governor, 88, 128–129; of Jayul, 83, 87; of Tsang, 127, 131
Guru Rinpoche. *See* Padmasambhava
Gya family of Ralung, xiv
Gyalse Chogtrul Jigme Tenzin Wangpo, xxix, 7
Gyalse Tenzin Rabgay, xxix, 7
Gyalwa Karmapa, 103
Gyalwa Tsongkhapa. *See* Tsongkhapa
Gyangtse, 128, 133–134, 155

hamlet: Gangtakha, xxviii, 29; Chuyur, 5, 17, 21
happiness, xv, xxiii, xxvii, 94
hell, 73, 84, 153, 164–165
hermitage, 36, 67, 87, 110, 112, 127, 163
Heruka Rupi Gyenchen, xv
Hinglila, 3, 40
homage, 22–23, 48–50, 106, 149, 160–161
humour, xii, xviii, xxii, xxxvi, 140
hypocrisy, xxvi–xxvii, 86, 161; attacking, xviii; canker, xxvi; condemn, xxvi–xxvii; deep-rooted, xxvi; destroy, 45; expose, xxvi; free of, 161; masked as truth, 45; religious, xxvi; veneer of, 86

identities, 46; misconceptions, xi
impermanence, xxviii

Jagarthang, 5, 26

Jamgon lineage, 169
Jamgon Trulku Mipham Chokyi Nyenjeth, 169
Jamtrul Rinpoche, 105, 107
Jatang Kunley, 45
Jiligang, 171
Jodod Ngotsha Lhacho Drolma, 111
Jomolhari, 109, 112
Jowo Shakyamuni, 137–138, 140

Kagyu, 2, 7, 143–144, 160, 162; lineage, 63, 92
Kagyupas, 144–145
Kagyu school, xii, 63, 90, 143–144, 162
Kagyu Serthreng, 63
Kara Buram Drangtsi Drolma, 111
karma: negative, 99, 153
Karmapa, xxxvi, 100–103
Kham, 107, 119
Khandro Yeshe Tshogyal. *See* Padmasambhava
Khyen Rabpa, 159
Kongpo, 118; Sumchogma of, xxxv
Kunga Legpa, 98, 138, 148, 150; foolery of, 120
Kunga Legpa Paljor Zangpo, 159
Kunga Zangpo, xv
Kunkhyen Longchen Rabjam. *See* Longchenpa
Kuntu Zangpo, Tibetan ruler, xiii–xiv
Kurje, 67–68, 70

Lady Mermaid, 96, 98–99
Lama Drukpa Kunley, 23, 51
Lama Kathogpa, xviii
Lama Ngawang Chogyal, xxx, 41, 64–65, 75–76, 79–80, 121–125, 167–168, 171–175
lamas, xxviii–xxx, 23, 29–31, 51, 54, 58, 64–65, 72, 75–76, 79–80, 122, 124–125, 167–168, 171–174
Lama Tshewang, xxviii–xxix, 29–31
Langdud, demon as dharma protector, 37
lay people, xxvii, 83–85, 124, 135, 159, 162
letters, 'ah'. *See* sacred letter
Lhacho Drolma. *See* Loleg Buthri
Lhasa, xxxii, 4, 118–119, 137, 142–145, 147–148, 152–153, 164; Drukpa Kunley address at market of, xxv
Lhomon, 2, 4, 9–10, 14, 70, *see also* Mon
liberation, 28, 41, 46, 48–49, 58, 61, 159, 165
The Life Story, Songs and Advices of Drukpa Kunley, xiii
Lobesa, 41
Lokthang Chamo, 47, 51
Loleg Buthri, 109–112
Longchenpa, 67, 70
Longrong Dudmo, water demoness, 44, 46–47
loose-leaf poti format, xiii
Lopon Kunzang Thinley, 90

Lord, 10, 45, 61, 70, 84, 90–91, 98–99, 115, 128, 134, 137
Lord Buddha, 45, 84, 134, 137
Lord of Death, 61, 91, 98–99, 128
Luetshogang. *See* Samtengang

Machig Labdron, 88
Machig Palha, 148–149
mad, xxxiii, 62; antics, 168, 173; antinomic, xxvii, 45; antithetical, xxvi; crazy, xvi, xviii, xxii, xxviii, 45, 49, 75, 145; eccentric, xxxi, 114, 153; foolery, 120, 147; heterodox, xxxii; idiosyncratic, 84; insane, xxxi, 134; lunacy, 120; maverick, xv–xvi, xxi, xxv, 83; non-conformist, xxvii; unconventional, xv, xxvi, xxxii, 79, 114
madman (myonpa), xi, xv, xxx, xxxiii, 79, 129, 134; of Tsang, xv, xxx; of Ue, xv
'madmen movement,' xv
Mahamudra, xxxii, 144
mahasiddha, xv, xxi
mani, 9, 22–23, 26, 120, 160, 175; badza guru, 70
manifestation, xxvi, 11, 73, 75, 160
Manjushri, 149n95
mantra, 9, 26, 68, 70
marketplace, xxvi, xxxvi, 70, 75–77, 142, 145, 150, 156
Marpa, saint 67

materialism, xxiii
meditation, 71–72, 76, 124, 153, 161, 163, *see also* devotion; prayer; worship
mendicant, xi, xv, xxviii, 64, 118, 159
Milarepa, saint/yogi 46, 63, 67, 160
minor lord, 115–116
Mipham Tshewang Tenzin (grandson of Drukpa Kunley). *See* Tshewang Tenzin
miracle man, xi, xix
miracles, xi, xvii–xix, 54, 70, 73, 133, 154; Arresting the Sun's Descent, 15; birth of goat-headed bull, 52–61; bones turn into live stag, 173; created small spring, 50; emerged from the pit, 42; family saw excrement for tormas, 166; herd of meat, 126–127, 129; like strand of hair, 4; pile of freshly harvested turnips, 17; poison had no effect on them, 69; skinning his scrotums, 14; torrent, 64, 106; Trashi Lhunpo's famed tea, 154–155, 157; twisted into a tight knot, 6; twists it into a knot, xviii, 118; undertaker who walks corpse 25–31; yogi who urinates gold, 62–65
Mon, 2, 4, 9–10, 14, 68, 70, 90, 124

monasteries, xxvi–xxvii; Arrow Notch/Datong Gonpa, 3; Daglha Gampo, 160–161; Dago Gonpa, 33–34; Dechenbu, 90; Dechenphu, 90; Drepung, 152–153; Drowolung, 67; Drukpa, 163; Gaden, 153; Gangchen Chophel, 156; Gelug, 143, 147, 153, 156, 162; Kagyu, 162; Ralung, 90, 124; Ramoche, 147, 149; Rinpung 27n38; Sacha, 155; Sera, 153; Tango, 7; Trashi Lhunpo, 156; Tsechen, 155; Zhalu, 159; Zolphu, 162
monks, 83–84, 102, 106, 122–123, 143–144, 148, 155, 160, 162; argumentative, 106; of Drepung, 152–153; immoral, 59; intoxicated, xv, 87–88; of Karmapa, 101; novice, 87; of Palkhor stupa, 135; of Ramoche, 147; of Sera, 153; unruly, 163
Monla Karchung, 67
Mon Paro, xxxiii
Monson, Elizabeth, xiii, xxxiii
More than a Madman, Monson and Tshering, xxxiii
mother, 17, 74; of all wisdom, 134; chiding of, 75; girls as, xxxvi; Only Mother, 148; Protector, 148
mountains, abodes of mountain deities, xx

Mount Kailash, 44–45, 71
musicians, 142, 145

Naga spirit, 46
Naljorpa. *See* yogi
namthars, xxxiv–xxxv, xxxviii;
   autobiography, xviii, xxxiv–
   xxxv; biography, xxxiii,
   147n91, 175n104
Nangkatse, 2, 7
Naropa, 63, 103
Needrup Zangpo, xvii, xxiv
Nepali renunciant, 160
ngagyal (pride), xxii, xxvii, 128,
   145
Ngawang Tenzin, 7
Nobgang village, 39
nomads, 4–5, 60, 142–143
nonduality; famed tea, 154–155,
   157; hunting dog symbolizes,
   14, 53, 171; no difference
   between chang and water,
   160; references, xxxiii, 72,
   86, 161; sexual union with a
   non-human, 46; urinated gold,
   xviii, 62–63, 65
nunnery, 79; Ralung, 80; *see also*
   monasteries
nuns, 36, 53, 59–60, 79–81, 91,
   101, 132, 160, 162
Nyapa Tshering, 96, 98–99
Nyingmapas, 142, 162
Nyingma school, 142, 162
Nyonpa Drukpa Kunley,
   'Breaking Ngawang Chogyal's
   Shackles of Avarice', 123

offerings, 29, 58–59, 70, 87, 124,
   132, 155, 163
Omniscient Buddha, 93
Onrey Dharma Singye, 90
Ön Rinpoche, 122–124
Onsa Chogyal Lingpa, governor
   of Jayul, 83
oral stories, xi, xxxiv, xxxvii

Pachang Namkha Drolma, 41,
   47, 53
Padmasambhava, xii, xvii, 29n39,
   36, 66n54, 67, 69–70, 98; as
   Guru Rinpoche, 41
Palden Lhamo deity, 2, 7, 81,
   148n93
Palkhor Stupa, 133
Palzang Buthri, xxxii, 137, 152
Palzang Dorji, 175
Panchen Lama, 156
Paro, xiv, xvii, xxviii–xxix, 5,
   13–14, 16, 21, 26–27, 29
patience, 138–140
Pelzang Butri, Bhutanese lady,
   xvi
Pema Lingpa, xiv–xv, xxx, 70–73
Phadampa Sangye, 88
Phajo Drukgom Zhigpo, *see*
   Padmasambhava
phallus-shaped weed, xxix
Phari, 4, 9
Phet, 88
philanderer, xi, xxxv
pilgrimage, xxvi, 142, 144–145, 163
Piwang Lingbu Dranyen Drolma,
   111

Potala, 51
practice, xiv, 61, 138–139, 145, 156; cherished, 72; dharma, 165; scene of devout, 160; spiritual, 54, 143; tantric, 101
practising patience, 137–140
pratyekabuddhas, 165n100
prayer, xii, xxix, 10, 21, 23, 30, 39, 48–50, 67
prejudices, xii, xviii, 75
Primordial Buddha, 63
prophecy, 7; cauldron could never be filled beyond that level, 157; Jamgon Trulku, lineage home of, 169; Lithang, good news from, 107; on rise of temple, 41; you stand to be more popular in the future, 103; your destiny lies in Lhomon, 2
Punakha, xiv, xxix, 3, 44, 167, 171

Rainbow body, xvii, xxxvi, 22
Ralung, xi, xiii–xiv, xxx–xxxi, xxxvi, 63–65, 75, 79–80, 122–124, 127, 129, 135
Rasa Thrulnang, 137
Rawa, 127–128
reality, awareness of, xvi
religious: hypocrisy, xiv, xxvi; institutions, xii, xv, xxiii, 167; lord, xi; practitioners, xxvi, 134
Rigden Norbu Dzoma, 4–7
Rinpung, xiv, 27, 119
ritual, 124, 167, 171

Sacha, 103, 105, 108–109, 155, 162
Sachu Melung Namkha Drolma, 110
sacred letter, 51, 68
saint (drubthob), xi–xii, xvii, 67, 73, 92, 103, 169
Sakyapas, 145
Sakya school, 144–145
Samantabhadra, 73
Samtengang, 53
Saraha, xxxi
savant, xi
Sekhar Guthog, 67
self-aggrandizement, xviii
self-arisen, 68
Semzangma, Lady, 2
Sera, 153
servant, 60, 93, 114–116, 161, 164
sex, xviii, xxi, xxvi–xxviii, xxxii, 57, 60, 79
sexual: advances, 109; connection, 68; discipline, xxxvi; exploits, xxxv; gestures, 171; intercourse, 46, 109, 164; laxity, xxi; misconduct, 79; prowess, 46, 68; relations, xxxv; themes, xxxviii
Sharmo Kunzangmo, 53
Sharna, in Paro, 5, 16–17
Shavaripa, xxxi, 102
Shingkarab, 5, 9, 13
shravakas, 165
Singye Gyeltshen, cave of, 36, 90
social critic, xi
Sojong, 155–156

songs, xi, xiii, xxxvii, 71, 87–88, 102, 127, 135, 148–149, 159, 162; about this beautiful girl, 102; bawdy, xviii; Bhutanese, 98; delightful, 87; dharma, 159; folk, 114, 145; humorous, xiv; licentious, xviii; philosophical, xxxv, 114; of praise, 148; satirical, xviii
Songtsen Gampo, 29, 137
spirits, xvii, xix–xx, 9, 17, 33–34, 54, 88, 171–172; *see also* demons
spiritual: commitments, xxvii, 85–86; life, xiv, xx; practice, 54, 143; prowess, xviii; realization, xv, 22, 173
spirituality, xvii–xviii
Stein, R.A., xiii
stupa, 15, 17, 135; black, 41; of Enlightenment 134n74; of Lord Buddha's Descent 134n74; of Miracles 134n74
sublime master, xi
Sumdar, 63–65
Sutras, 71, 87

Tagzik Domdrey Dugdrul Drolma, 111
takin, 52–61
Tales of a Mad Yogi, Monson, xxxiii
Talo village, 39
Tango, xvi
Tango University, 7
tantras, 58, 87

temples, 13, 67; Jampa Lhakhang, Bhutan, 29; Jampa Lhakhang, Tibet, 105; Jokhang, 137; Jowo Shakyamuni, 137; Khyimay Lhakhang, 41; Kyerchu Lhakhang, 29; Monsib Lhakhang, 70; Taktshang (Tiger's Nest Temple), xviii
tent dwellers, 87
Tenzin, 47
Terton Pema Lingpa, xxx, 70–73
thangka, 63–65
Thimphu. *See* Wang
Tibetan, xxvi, 10–11, 54, 56, 63–64, 88, 122; saints, xxix, 63; wanderer, 21–22, 65
Tilopa, 63, 103
timug (mental stupor), 144–145
Toep Chandana, 3; *see also* Toep Lungdram Wogma
Toep Tshewang, 3–6
Toepa Tshewang, 6, 176
tormas, 166–168
Trashi Lhunpo, 156–157
travellers, 9–11, 13–14, 142
Tremola Pass, 4
Tsang, xv, xxx, 79, 127, 131, 156
Tsang Desi, 126–127, 129, 131
Tsang Nyon Heruka or the Madman of Tsang, xxx
Tsangpa Gyare, 90–91
Tsang province, 90, 127, 133
Tsechen, 127, 156
Tshelungna, 41
Tshering Wangyal, 42

Tshewang Tenzin, xvi, xxxiii, 7
Tsondru Zangmo, 176
Tsongkhapa, 146–149
Tsunchung Tashi, 176

ultimate reality, xvi
Ü Nyon Kunga Zangpo or the Madman of Ü, xxx
urinate, 5, 62–63, 65

Vajradhara, 63, 103
Vajrayana, 22, 54; teachings of, 61
virtues, 72, 92–94
virtuous leadership, 94
vows, 58, 60, 83, 85–86, 155; full ordination, 159; mental, 101; moral, xxvi, 134–135; novice, 159; primary, 156; subsidiary, 156; Three, 87, 149, 161

Wachen Bumo Goeked Palzom, 53
wanderer:
wanderer/wandering, 23–24, 66, 88, 123; carefree, 87, 90; mendicant, xi; purposeless, 44; Tibetan, 21–22, 65; yogi, 110
Wang, xiv, xxxiii, 5, 41–42, 90; Danglo village in, 3
Wang Barma, 3, 39, 42, 101

Wang ceremony 101, 102n66
Wangdi, 5, 40
Wangza Chozom, 41, 53
water bodies, residences of water spirits, xx
Wencheng, Princess, 137
Wodod Drak, 5, 9, 13; cave of, 5, 9, 13
Wola Gyap Tenzin, 43, 47, 49–51
Wolakha in Bhutan, 44, 47, 50
women, xxix, xxxv, 96, 101, 114
worship, 45, 58; *see also* devotion

xylographic prints, xiii

Yamdro lake, 2, 96–99
Yamdro Nangkartse, 127
Yamdro province, 2, 96
Yangpachen, 101
Yarlung dynasty, 29
yogi (naljorpa), xi, xxxiii–xxxiv, 21, 23, 46, 68, 70, 84, 111, 116, 118, 159, 162–165

Zhabdrung Ngawang Namgyal, xii, 7, 27n38
zhedang as tshenyi, 143
Zhenlog Choje Sachab Drolma, 111
Zhingchong Drukdra, 81

About the Author

Needrup Zangpo studied English, Indian and Greek literature in college. He taught himself research skills and the art and craft of journalism while working in Bhutan's civil service and emerging media for two decades. He lives in Thimphu, Bhutan's capital, studying and meditating on Buddhist literature in classical Tibetan, as well as Bhutanese culture, history and literary traditions.

HarperCollins *Publishers* India

At HarperCollins India, we believe in telling the best stories and finding the widest readership for our books in every format possible. We started publishing in 1992; a great deal has changed since then, but what has remained constant is the passion with which our authors write their books, the love with which readers receive them, and the sheer joy and excitement that we as publishers feel in being a part of the publishing process.

Over the years, we've had the pleasure of publishing some of the finest writing from the subcontinent and around the world, including several award-winning titles and some of the biggest bestsellers in India's publishing history. But nothing has meant more to us than the fact that millions of people have read the books we published, and that somewhere, a book of ours might have made a difference.

As we look to the future, we go back to that one word— a word which has been a driving force for us all these years.

Read.